Legends

Conversations with
Baseball Greats

Legends
Conversations with
Baseball Greats

Art Rust, Jr.
with
Michael Marley

McGraw-Hill Publishing Company
New York St. Louis San Francisco Auckland Bogota
Hamburg London Madrid Mexico Milan Montreal
New Delhi Paris São Paulo Singapore Sydney
Tokyo Toronto

1 2 3 4 5 6 7 8 9 DOC DOC 8 9 2 1 0 9

ISBN 0-07-054300-3

Book design by Mark Bergeron

To my darling Edna,
who was always with me

Contents

Preface

Joseph Paul DiMaggio, Jackie Roosevelt Robinson, Walter Lanier "Red" Barber. My heart starts racing every time I hear these names. It is probably no accident that all three come from the world of baseball. I have always been a sports fan, but baseball is my great love.

The first major league game I remember seeing was in 1935 in the Polo Grounds with my father. The New York Giants versus the Boston Braves. Babe Ruth was in his last season, ending his career as a player with the Braves. From the right-field stands I saw the Babe and other great stars: Rabbit Maranville, Mel Ott, Carl Hubbell, Shanty Hogan, Wally Berger, Danny McFayden, Bill Terry, Hal Schumacher. I was totally captivated.

Actually, I had become a baseball fan two years earlier, in 1933, when my father and Uncle Johnny were listening to a radio broadcast of the World Series games between the New York Giants and the Washington Senators. I had lived in Manhattan for all of my young life, so naturally I was a Giants fan. But what really captivated me that day in 1933 were the names coming out of the speaker: "Fat Freddie" Fitzsimmons, "Tarzan" Roy Parmelee, JoJo Moore, Ossie Bluege, Goose Goslin, Heinie Manush.

I also became a St. Louis Cardinals fan. My allegiance

to the Cards dates to 1937. Joe "Ducky" Medwick won the triple crown that year. I had heard my father speak affectionately of the Cardinals, and Medwick's feat pulled me into their camp.

The same year, 1937, I got scarlet fever and was quarantined in my room. While "incarcerated," I picked up the habit of listening to Earl Harper broadcasting the Newark Bear games on radio station WNEW. The Bears were a farm team of the New York Yankees in the Triple A International League. In 1937 they had without question the greatest minor league club in history. They won the pennant that year by 25½ games over the Montreal Royals, piloted by Rabbit Maranville. They were blessed with players like "King Kong" Charlie Keller, Bob "Suitcase" Seeds, Joe "Flash" Gordon, Atley Donald, Joe Beggs, and Vito Tamulis.

My love affair with radio and baseball started in 1938 when I listened to the World Series between the Yankees and the Chicago Cubs. Three networks broadcast that series, Mel Allen on one, Bob Elson on the second, and Red Barber on the third. Walter Lanier "Red" Barber was absolutely inspirational. He could paint word pictures like no one else. As far as I'm concerned, he was the greatest baseball play-by-play guy who ever lived. When I heard him, I knew what I wanted to do for a living.

I graduated from Long Island University in 1949. At that time becoming a sports announcer was almost impossible for a black. I intended to be a doctor. My medical adventure ended when I witnessed an autopsy for the first time and fainted dead away. A career in medicine did not seem feasible.

Meanwhile, I met the real love of my life, Edna Hayes, in January, 1951, at a sorority dance at the Savoy Ballroom. Edna was attending Hunter College. We became engaged in August, 1951, right after the Kid Gavilan-Billy Graham welterweight championship fight (Gavilan won a controversial

Preface

decision). Edna and I married in September of 1952. We coauthored five books together and one beautiful daughter, Suzanne, who arrived on April 11, 1964. Suzanne graduated from Sarah Lawrence in June of 1986. My darling Edna was stricken by a cerebral aneurysm on January 23, 1986 in New Orleans during Super Bowl Week. She died on February 6, 1986. I have not been the same since that day.

Back to the world of work—Jocko Maxwell was the first black sportscaster. He was on WWRL, 1600 on the AM dial. I auditioned for him and went to work for WWRL in 1954. Fourteen years later I switched to NBC TV. By 1975 reading the scores on TV had become boring. I had always wanted to do a sports talk show, and in 1981 I got my chance with WABC. The rest, as they say, is history. "Art Rust, Jr.'s Sports Talk Show" has become a fixture at 770 on your AM radio dial. The "conversations" with the players in this book reflect my fifty-five-year love affair with the great American pastime. I hope you find the same interest and fascination I do with the words of these baseball greats.

1

Red
Barber

THE year was 1938. That was the first time I ever "heard" Walter Lanier (Red) Barber. Along with Mel Allen and Bob Elson, he did play-by-play of the Chicago Cubs-New York Yankees World Series. Each man worked on a different network. To me, Red Barber was the greatest baseball announcer who ever lived.

I can still hear him bellowing from the radio speaker now. "The bases are F.O.B." (meaning full of Brooklyns), or "Dolph Camilli hits a Bedford Avenue blast." That meant a home run in the language I call Barberese. When things really got exciting, he'd yell, "Oh, doctor!" Yes, Red Barber painted you a picture. I mean he made you see a game on the radio.

You felt as though you were in the ballpark when he described those epic Brooklyn Dodger-St. Louis Cardinal ballgames. It was Whitlow Wyatt against Mort Cooper or Luke Hamlin against Howie Pollet.

Sometimes, I'd sit in the farthest corner of the Polo Grounds, with no one around me, and I'd actually do play-by-play like Red Barber. He made me want to paint the pictures the way he did. Over the years now I've gotten to know Red. I first met him in 1955 and I was awestruck. The only guys I've ever met who made my toes curl are

Legends

Red Barber and Joseph Paul DiMaggio. Both of them have been such a chunk of my life.

Rust: Red, the first time I remember hearing your name I was listening to the 1938 Chicago Cubs-New York Yankees World Series. I heard you—I heard Bob Elson, out of Chicago—I heard Mel Allen. I didn't realize at the time that three different networks were doing that World Series. What's your recollection of that World Series?

Barber: Well, that World Series was broadcast on NBC, in the east, CBS, and Mutual. In other words, in those days it was not exclusive. The first exclusive broadcast of a World Series, Art, was in 1939, when Gillette bought the rights and put them on Mutual.

Rust: Cincinnati and the Yankees.

Barber: Yes, that's right. Ah, my recollection of the 1938 series—the one that you listened to when you recall hearing me for the first time—was that the Yankees were a tremendously efficient team and that they were almost a cold team in precision. They had everything. They had pitching, they had great fielding—it was very hard to get a ball out of the infield—and of course they had power. That was a hallmark. As far as remembering things, you remember in the second game when the second base umpire, "Uncle Charley" Moran, was hit in the mouth with a thrown ball by second baseman Joe Gordon?

Rust: Yes, I remember that.

Barber: And it really shattered his mouth and his teeth, but the old man—it had knocked his cap off—he stood there, white-haired, but he wouldn't go down, and then he wouldn't go out of the game.

Rust: What about the heroic pitching job by Jerome Herman "Dizzy" Dean?

Barber: Well, that's what I was coming up to. In the next game, which was in Chicago, game three, Dizzy Dean had a bad arm. He had hurt his arm after Earl Averill hit a ball back in an All-Star game in Washington in 1937 that broke his toe, and he returned to pitching too soon and with a foreign motion. He hurt his arm in Boston, and he was never fast again. So that afternoon in Chicago, Dean had nothing left but just a slow . . . just a slow curveball. But he had a great deal of courage and, but for a silly error when his shortstop, Billy Jurges, and his third baseman, Stanley Hack, both very good professionals. . . .

Rust: Ran into one another, yeah. . . .

Barber: They ran together and the ball that Lou Gehrig had hit, a ground ball, instead of being an out went into the outfield for a base hit. Dean might have gone into the ninth inning, but as it was, he got beat.

Rust: Red, you started with Larry MacPhail in Cincinnati in 1934. Tell me about that.

Barber: There isn't much to tell, Art, or there's a lot to tell. I was on an educational radio station at Gainesville, Florida, WRUF, at the university. A daylight-operated station, no commercials. I had been to Cincinnati three different times at my own expense, taking auditions and wearing my white linen suit. Of course, you couldn't audition for a baseball game in those days because the Cincinnati stations didn't broadcast them. But I had been up there and had done well in the auditions, and then when

3

Legends

MacPhail was brought in by the bank ... Sidney Weill was an automobile dealer in Cincinnati and he owned the ballclub. People today, unless they are our ages, don't remember that we had a tremendous Depression going on. Banks were being closed and people were losing their businesses, and Sidney Weil went bankrupt. The bank wanted to get out from under the ballclub, and they turned to Branch Rickey in St. Louis and asked if he would come and run the Cincinnati team. Rickey said no. But Rickey recommended Larry MacPhail, who had worked for him at Columbus in the American Association, and the bank brought in MacPhail and told him to, you know, to get them out of the baseball business. MacPhail turned to about the only man in Cincinnati who had much money, Powell Crosley, Jr., who owned WLW, which was then a half-a-million-watt transmitter. Mr. Crosley was also a manufacturer of refrigerators and radio sets. He bought controlling interest in the ballclub. So then, Mr. Crosley had, in addition to WLW, a station called WSAI, which was five thousand watts, and he said, "As long as I've got a baseball team and two radio stations, at least I should put some ball games on my smaller station." He asked if they had anybody on the staff who could do baseball, and the answer was no. The chief announcer said, "Well, that boy from Florida has been up here and he has done well—you remember the fellow in the white linen suit." And they said, yeah, they remembered the white linen suit. I got a call then on the fourth of March in 1934—I remember the date quite clearly—and they said would I come to Cincinnati to do Reds' games for twenty-five dollars a week. I answered immediately that I would come and the next day I was on a bus to Tampa, Florida, to spring training camp. I stayed there a week, went up to Cincinnati and waited for the ballclub. So that is how I got to Cincinnati. And I never met MacPhail until I got to Cincinnati.

4

Red Barber

Rust: You know, speaking of the '34 Reds, my father's favorite ballplayer was the first sacker—he used to wear his hat on the side—Sunny Jim Bottomley.

Barber: Yes, Jim Bottomley was the first baseman at Cincinnati then. And he always had this big smile—that was his trademark. He had a happy disposition, but it was a genuine smile, and it reflected his outlook on life.

Rust: All right, Red—what are some of the principles that you adhered to doing ballgames, as far as integrity, honesty, and so on.

Barber: You're talking . . . well, I'll tell you, Art, somehow or other, I never cared who won or who lost the ballgame. I felt it my job—and you have to remember this was on radio—I felt that my job was to report to people who couldn't see the event what was happening. Certainly I had no right as one individual to have any wishes on the air, any interest in winning or losing, as compared to the thousands, and at times, millions of people who were listening in and couldn't see it. Each of them had a favorite player or a team that they wanted; in other words, they had their own reasons for their reactions. My job was, in essence, to report the game. The great umpire, Bill Klem, used to say that there is nothing to umpiring—you umpire the ball. In other words, the ball is either fair or foul. The ball either gets to first base before the runner or it doesn't. And it's either a ball or a strike. So I tried to broadcast that way.

Rust: All right, Red, we heard you in 1939. You were the top banana. Big Al Helfer was the second banana. What are your memories of 1939, your first year with Brooklyn?

Barber: I arranged for Station WOR to run a cable onto the field with a microphone and I got fifteen extra minutes. I invited New York Giant Manager Bill Terry and Brooklyn

Legends

Dodger skipper Leo Durocher to be my pre-game guests. They both talked about their batting orders, their pitching, how they were going to run their clubs, and what kind of year they expected. Everybody was talking about that pre-game show. It got me off to a great start. Prior to that Dodger opening day at Ebbets Field, I got a little, shall we say, burned up by an article in *Time Magazine*. *Time* had a little story about the advent of play-by-play broadcasting coming into New York. You will remember, Art, that the Yankees and the Giants and the Dodgers were opposed to radio play-by-play. They were fearful that it would hurt their attendance. They had illegal contracts, because they did not allow any of their home games to be broadcast—even Western Union recreations anywhere—for five years starting in 1934. MacPhail, when he came to Brooklyn in '38, made up his mind he was not going to renew the deal. McDonald and Allen did the Yankees and Giants home games only. And McPhail said that he was going to broadcast, and so he forced the Giants and the Yankees to go on the air. Well, MacPhail knew of my work in Cincinnati. And I had been on several World Series, so he insisted with General Mills, the sponsors, that I come into Brooklyn. I was brought to Brooklyn, and then the Giants and Yankees were home, and General Mills selected for them Arch MacDonald, who did the Washington Senators games.

Rust: Him and Mel Allen—Allen was the second banana.

Barber: Well, the second, or third, or fourth—they had a lot of them running around there then—depending on whether it was the Yankees or the Giants. You can hardly tell who was who, and J. C. Flippen was around, and this, that, and the other thing. What I am trying to say is that *Time Magazine* had a story about the broadcasting of play-by-play baseball and they devoted their story to the Giants and the Yankees and to Arch MacDonald. They gave him the feature, including a picture. They didn't even mention

Brooklyn or Barber. Well, you can imagine that didn't set too well with me. So I determined that I was not only going to be an excellent broadcaster at Brooklyn, and do all that I could, but that on opening day I was really going to splurge.

Rust: You know, Red, I was at the ballpark with my late friend Georgie Vaz when you did the first ... I believe you were doing the first television thing. You were holding up the products. We were sitting right behind you. What are your memories of that day?

Barber: Well, Art, I tell you, you can have a great many memories of it. NBC had an experimental TV station, and the man who was running it was Alfred H. "Doc" Morton, Vice President of The National Broadcasting Company, and Morton, early in the summer, had a baseball game on— Princeton at Columbia, a college game—and they had Bill Stern announcing it. Morton asked me to come by and see him and he said, "Red, I would like the best in the world to get a major league ballgame on our television station, but I know that if I go to the Yankees or the Giants, they are so opposed to radio and to broadcasting, they won't even let me talk to them. I know I have no chance to get one of their games on television. I understand that MacPhail can be very difficult at times, and I don't know how to approach him. I have never met him, and I would not like to go see him and be a failure. Would you, as a favor to me—I had known Morton off and on slightly for a couple of years— would you as a favor to me, ask MacPhail to grant permission to let us do any of his ballgames at Brooklyn?" Well, you know MacPhail was the first man to fly a big league ballclub and he was the first man that put in lights.

Rust: Right, in '35.

Barber: He was the first man to put in a season ticket plan. He was the first man to do so many original things. He and Branch Rickey brought baseball into modern times.

7

Legends

When I went in to see MacPhail, I said, "Larry, do you want another first?" He said, "Yes. What is it?" I said, "to do the first big league ballgame on television." He said, "Sure." So I put him on the phone with Morton and I think—this will show you how times have changed, Art—MacPhail said to Morton, "I've got this doubleheader on Saturday in August with Cincinnati here, and it'll be sold out. You can do the first game, but," he said, "I want something for this. I want you to install in the press room a receiving set."

I don't think there were a hundred TV receiving sets in New York then in 1939. Receiving sets, Art, you lifted up the top—it was on a hinge—and inside the top, under the top was a big mirror and the tubes sat in the sets pointing straight up. What you saw was the reflection from the tube in that big mirror. So Morton agreed. A set was installed on Friday night and NBC very carefully took it away on Sunday morning. But that was the first TV for a sporting event in the history of television.

Rust: And I was there! Of course I didn't see it on television. You were actually holding up the products.

Barber: Well, you see, we had three sponsors that year— we had Ivory Soap, Socony Vacuum, and Wheaties. To my knowledge, they were the first commercials that were ever on television. And of course there was no rehearsal. There were no cue cards, and there were only two cameras. One was on ground level, back of home plate; the other was in the upper third-base stands, where you were sitting, and the camera was right back there with the fans. I was sitting right there alongside the camera, along with the fans. So, what we did was when the time came to do the Ivory Soap commercial, I just held up a bar of Ivory Soap and I talked a little bit about Ivory Soap. You know, how pleasant it was, and 99, or something else percent, pure—that was the commercial. When the time came to do Socony Vacuum, I

8

put on a Mobil gas service-station attendant's cap, held up a can of Mobil Oil, and talked about that a little bit, and that was that commercial. But we went all out for Wheaties. You may recall that for Wheaties, we shook some Wheaties into a bowl, sliced a banana, sprinkled a little sugar on, and poured on some milk, and said, "This is the breakfast of champions."

Rust: That's fantastic, Red. But Red Barber is "tearing up the peapatch," "walking in tall cotton," "F.O.B.," "oh, doctor"—how did those come about?

Barber: I never planned, Art, to, you know, to come up with any of those expressions. Naturally, we are all creatures of our heredity and our environment. I had heard expressions like that. "F.O.B." is the only one I coined. The others I had heard and picked up and just used.

Rust: For those who don't know, "walking in tall cotton" means what? Pitcher in trouble, right?

Barber: Oh, it means that everything is fine, because the cotton is growing very well.

Rust: Oh, I see, yeah.

Barber: There's gonna be a bountiful crop.

Rust: Who was the greatest pitcher and the greatest hitter that you ever saw, Red?

Barber: I would think—I would think, Art, that maybe the pitcher that I thought the most of was . . . if I had to select one pitcher to pitch one game and my life hung on it, I'd pick Carl Hubbell. And as far as a great hitter—well, when you define hitter there are so many things that go into it. Let's say that the best all-around ballplayer that I saw—and that includes hitting, fielding, running, and everything else; I'd rather answer it that way—would be Willie Mays.

Rust: Red, could you name your all-time team?

Barber: I have never done that, Art. I have never made a prediction of how a game would come out. I have never felt that way. I have never made a prediction about who would win a pennant. I have never talked that way. My business, as I said earlier, was to describe the ballgame and mostly not to be involved, and I have never picked football scores. I know that a lot of broadcasters in the past would have programs, especially on Friday evenings, when they would run down a list of the college games. I have always stayed away from that—I never did it—for the same reason that I never picked an all-star team.

Rust: Red, what's your evaluation of big Ernie Lombardi?

Barber: I would say that Lombardi really had more ability to put the bat on the baseball than most any other hitter in the history of baseball. Maybe you'd put him in a class with Ted Williams. Lombardi was so pitifully slow. He was probably the slowest runner that we ever had. The infield always played back in the outfield for him, and yet Lombardi twice was the batting champion. His ability, as I said, to put the bat on the ball was simply superb.

Rust: What about him defensively?

Barber: An excellent catcher. After all, he caught Johnny Vander Meer's two no-hit ballgames.

Rust: That's right, in 1938. You remember how they used to play him—everybody played him on the edge of the outfield grass. Red, about those Western Union ballgames. Tell us about that. I used to hear them, and—what exactly, what information did you receive and how much embellishment did you have to do?

Barber: Well, now—I'm gonna, I'm gonna explain a little bit about that, Art, but also I'd like to say that in a book that I wrote—it came out in 1970, called "The Broadcaster"—it has a whole chapter about how we did the Western Union Paragraph One games. Nobody went on the road with the ballclub, unless it would be maybe for one or two games for a special reason, because line charges were too much. And so there wasn't the money in broadcasting. We were still in those days coming out of the Depression. MacPhail was the first man to have all of his ballgames done live. When he came out of the Army, he and Del Webb bought the Yankees. It was MacPhail in 1946 who put the Yankee road games on the air. He took Mel Allen on the road—that's the first time that that happened.

But as far as Western Union was concerned, they had a standard service. It was called Paragraph One. Western Union had an exclusive on all of the sixteen major league teams. And they had a specialist, a sending operator who stayed at each of those parks and he sent each game out. He would send the weather. He would send the line-ups and he would send the umpires. Then he would send the name of the first batter, just say Smith up—and then B-1-L—ball one low; S-1-C—strike one called; FB—fouled back. He wouldn't even put down strike 2; it would be up to you to know that it was strike 2. Then he would say out, fly to right—no names outside of the names of the batter and the names of the pitcher and the catcher—it was up to the announcer in the studio with that skeleton to put the flesh on the bones.

Rust: And you did it, and you did it very well.

Barber: When I was broadcasting a game that I could see for myself, I would broadcast it with my eyes. And when I was in the studio, I broadcast these out-of-town games from a series of mental pictures. I had mentally photographed every player in the league—that was my business to do that. I had pictures and dimensions of all of the ballparks, and I stood in the studio with the operator and the associate broadcaster, and we were the only ones there. The engineer would be in the control room back of a glass panel—he wasn't in the studio. And in that studio I always stood, because if you sat down, you'd be liable to get sleepy. When standing you can move a little bit and twist and you can keep more awake and stay on your toes, and so I stood. I used a music rack that I would turn flat for a scorebook, and I would look over the shoulder of the Western Union receiving operator. I deliberately had the sound of the Western Union dot/dash equipment over the air as well as the Western Union operator's typewriter.

Rust: I recall that.

Barber: I wanted the listeners to know that I was not at the game—that I was doing a re-creation. I was doing the best re-creation I could, but I was not responsible for something I did not see. And so when the wire went out, which it often did, I just immediately said, "well, the wire's out"—and I think the listeners were quite happy. I always believed in complete honesty. That was its own reward, and I never had a complaint about people saying that they knew that I was doing a wire report.

Rust: Red, in 1947, "The Year When All Hell Broke Loose"—the title of your most recent book—let's talk about Jack Roosevelt Robinson, and your reactions when Rickey told you he was going to sign a black ballplayer.

Barber: (Laughter) You just gave the title of that book.

Rust: That's right.

Barber: Let me say about that book, Art, it's one of the things that has given me the most satisfaction in my life, because I knew so much of what was going on, and so much of it has been forgotten by people. I feel that in writing that book, that I have written an American history book.

Rust: No doubt about it.

Barber: There is material in that book that people won't find anywhere else, and everything in that book is absolutely accurate. In World War II, I was a fund-raising chairman in the Borough of Brooklyn for the American Red Cross for two years and I had Branch Rickey as my public relations man. I had him working for me at the Red Cross. And in the second year of this fund raising, I also was fund-raising chairman for the entire City of New York. So, Mr. Rickey was busy and I was busy. Late in March of 1945, we had a Red Cross meeting at Brooklyn Borough President John Cashmore's office in Borough Hall. With volunteers, you know, you have to let them talk; and they were all talking, so it was well into the afternoon when the meeting broke up. Mr. Rickey and I went around the corner to Joe's Restaurant, a very famous restaurant there in Brooklyn, near Borough Hall, a landmark. Nobody was in there but a few waiters, and we went to a corner way in the back. Mr. Rickey had something on his mind, and it wasn't the Red Cross. He looked around to be sure that there was no one who was close who could hear what he said, and he said to me, "I am going to bring a Negro player to the Brooklyn Dodgers." Well, you can imagine my surprise, because baseball was an all-white enterprise.

Well, anyhow, what Mr. Rickey said was, "When I was a young man at Ohio Wesleyan University, I was a baseball coach, and I took my team to South Bend, Indiana, for a series with Notre Dame. In those days the clerk at the hotel desk just pushed the register out, and you came up and you signed it. My catcher, Charles Thomas, came up—he was a Negro boy, and he was my best player—he came up and when he started to sign the register, the clerk jerked the register away and said, "We do not register Negroes in this hotel." And he said it in a very loud voice, to be heard all over the lobby. I said, "You don't understand. We are the Ohio Wesleyan Baseball Team. We're going against the University of Notre Dame. This is my catcher."

And the clerk immediately said, "I don't care who you are. I don't care who he is or why you are here—we do not register Negroes in this hotel, and that is that." I was stunned, and then I said to the clerk, "Now, I've got two beds in my room." And the clerk said, "Yes." And I said, "Well, now if this young man doesn't register, is it all right if he shares the room with me?" And the clerk very pleasantly said, "Well, I guess so." So Rickey said, "Give me the key to the room." And he took the key and he handed it over to his catcher and said, "Now you go up to the room and you wait for me until I get the rest of the team settled and then I'll be coming up."

And Mr. Rickey said, "When I opened the door, there was this splendid young man, and he was sitting on the edge of a chair and he was just pulling at his hands, and he was crying. His heart was broken, and he said, 'Mr. Rickey, it's my skin—it's my skin. If I could just tear it off I'd be just like everyone else.' "

And Rickey said to me this March afternoon at Joe's Restaurant, that all these years he had heard the sobs of this young man. "And year after year I have been intending to do something about it. I am now in my middle sixties and if I am going to do anything about it, I'm going to have to do it now. Mrs. Rickey and my children are absolutely opposed to my doing this. They say that my health is not good and that I am too old and that every hand will be against me, and in the newspapers, they will vilify me. But," said Mr. Rickey, "I am going to do it." And he said, "Now I have already set my plans in motion. I have told the Board

14

of Directors; they know about it. Mrs. Rickey and my family, they know about it, and now you know about it, and you are free to tell your wife, but she is not to tell anyone and you are the only people who will know about it. I have put a team in the Negro leagues." In those days, Art, as our listeners may not know, we had Negro baseball in leagues. "I put a team in the Negro leagues which is called the Brooklyn Brown Dodgers; and when the white Dodgers are on the road, the Brown Dodgers will play at Ebbets Field. I have sent my three best scouts out to look at all of the Negro players, scouting for the best Negro player that they can find." And he said, "All of their reports will come to me at 215 Montague Street. But I am scouting for a Negro player who has the physical ability to break the color line, and when I find him, I am going to do it."

So the reports kept coming in and Jackie Robinson's name kept coming up more and more frequently as the player with the ability. Mr. Rickey never laid eyes on Robinson as a player when this procedure was going on. So then, when he determined from these reports that Robinson seemed to be the player with the physical gifts to do it, he sent Clyde Sukeforth out to Chicago. Robinson was with the Kansas City Monarchs; they were in Chicago for a series, but Robinson was unable to play then. He had a bad shoulder; he was going to be out for three or four days. Sukeforth went to Chicago to bring Robinson to Brooklyn to Mr. Rickey's office.

And in Mr. Rickey's office, Mr. Rickey told Robinson that he wasn't there as a prospect for the Brown Dodgers, he was there as a prospect for the white Dodgers. And then Mr. Rickey went over for two hours all of the problems that Robinson would face. Mr. Rickey did not use profanity, but that morning he told Robinson everything that would be said to him—everything—every curse, every invective, just about everything. Mr. Rickey was a very intelligent man and intelligently vocal. He laid it out for Robinson.

I know that as time went by and things would happen on the field, Robinson would laugh and tell me, "that wasn't no surprise. Mr. Rickey told me that that was going to happen." And so, Mr. Rickey, because he had to test Robinson spiritually, said, "if you want to be the first Negro player in the big leagues, you will—I know you are very competitive—but you will have to promise me that for three years you will not answer back, no matter what is said to you, no matter what is done to you. You will take it. You will not answer back."

In effect, in the words of the Bible, you will turn the other cheek. And as Mr. Rickey said later, he kept turning his cheek and turning his cheek until he didn't have any cheeks left. They were all beat off. But Robinson said when Mr. Rickey finally got to the point—when Mr. Rickey said, "Do you think you can do it?" Robinson said, "Mr. Rickey, I've got to do it."

And of course, as we know, he did it. But people I think have forgotten the enormous pressure put on him. Can you imagine, Art, for three years, Jackie Robinson—and Rickey used to say he was the most competitive man since Ty Cobb—for three years, he never said a word back.

Rust: Red, let me ask you one question. How much soul searching—you're from Mississippi now—how much soul searching did Red Barber have to do when Rickey told you this?

Barber: This came to me as a shock. I came home to my wife and told her about it, and I said, "I don't know, I may have to quit, and I don't know whether I can go through with it." And she said, "Well you don't have to quit tonight. Let's have a martini and then let's have dinner." As time went by, I began to do some very serious tough analysis.

16

One, it was apparent that then I had the best sports announcing job in the world, and I'd helped to create it; and if I walked away from that, what was I going to do? That came first.

Rust: A matter of economics.

Barber: That's right. And then I realized that I had had nothing to say about the parents I was born to. I had nothing to say that by accident of birth I happened to be born white, and therefore, what have I got to be so high and mighty about over somebody of another color? And that helped. But then—in my books I have written a good deal about my first World Series in 1935 and what Judge Landis said before the first game. The essence of it was that he said, "You fellows, you broadcasters, I know you're very good and you know your business, but these ballplayers are very good, and I don't want you to try to play ball with them. You are to report what they do. These managers are very good. Don't try to second-guess them; don't try to manage. You just report what they do. The umpires are very efficient; don't, for goodness sake, second-guess them. You report what they do. Report everything you can see. Just report," he said, "report. By report I mean, suppose a ballplayer walks over to my box and spits in my face. Don't feel sorry for the commissioner, just report what happens and report my reaction, if I have one. Gentlemen, leave your opinions in your hotel rooms, and report." And that really has been the foundation of my broadcasting philosophy all through the years. And, you know, the psychiatrists say there is nothing stronger than the voice that comes from the grave.

Judge Landis was dead by the time that Rickey broke the color line. The Commissioner then was Happy Chandler. But I heard that old white-haired man's voice when I was examining myself in my torment because I was troubled, of course I was troubled. And I don't mince matters about it at all. And I heard Landis, and then all of a sudden I said to myself, "For goodness sakes, I'm not Branch Rickey, I'm not Robinson, I'm not the other ball players. I'm not involved. But what is my job? My job in this procedure is merely to report—and that's all I ever did."

Rust: Red, you did a helluva job.

2

Joe DiMaggio

IN trying to capsulize the careers of the great ones, the tendency in sports is to resort to a recitation of numbers. Mention Babe Ruth and someone says 714. Bring up Ted Williams and someone is sure to recall his .406 batting average from 1941. Start rapping about Muhammad Ali and they'll say he was the three-time world heavyweight champion.

Well, Joseph Paul DiMaggio's name brings numbers to mind, too. Numbers like 2,214 total career hits and his three MVP Awards. Or the fact that, in thirteen lucky big-league seasons, he played for ten pennant winners and nine World Series champions.

The magic number associated with DiMaggio, of course, is 56, the remarkable and record hitting streak he had in '41. But mere numbers are hardly the measure of a man like DiMaggio; to me, he's magic.

When I was born, it seemed like F.D.R. was president, LaGuardia was Mayor of New York, Joe Louis was here, and DiMaggio was there. He made everything look so easy. He was elegance in Yankee pinstripes. He was so damn nonchalant!

He was and is part of my life. And I was a Cardinal fan! But we all tend to cling to part of our boyhood, to our

*past. Perhaps if I had been eight or nine years old in '51—
when Willie Mays came up—he'd mean that much to me.
I'll never forget the 56-game streak. I hung on every pitch.
I was so depressed when he stopped. The man has a lasting
charisma. Of all the guests I've ever interviewed, only two
brought me to tears. One was Red Barber, the other Joseph
Paul DiMaggio.*

Rust: First thing I always think about when someone says
"Joseph Paul DiMaggio" is the first World Series game I
saw—Game Two, 1936 Series, Giants-Yankees at the Polo
Grounds and the Yankees win it, 18-4—Lazzeri off Dick
Coffman, home run, opposite field, the bases totally pop-
ulated. That was the game where Gomez stopped to watch
the airplane fly over. The highlight of my life was Hank
Lieber hitting a tremendous wallop to Joseph Paul. And you
caught the ball on the cinder path.

You ran halfway up the clubhouse stairs and you realized, hey, President Roosevelt is still here. Tell me about
that.

DiMaggio: We were leading by such a big score, and the
President did stay there for the whole ballgame. There was
an announcement made, "Please do not leave the ballpark
until the last out because we're going to get the President's
car from the centerfield gate and bring it over to the stands.
And after he leaves in the car, you can all disperse." Well,
when I made the catch, I started up the stairway to the
clubhouse.

Rust: Then you remembered.

DiMaggio: Yes, and then I remembered. Right, I stopped
on the second step. So he came by, and he had that fedora

on his head—this is President Roosevelt we're talking about and he always had that fedora hat and that cigarette holder with the long cigarette—and as he came by, he doffed his hat at me. You know, he was acknowledging, "Nice catch."

Rust: I'll never forget that.

DiMaggio: And I won't, either.

Rust: Then I think about little Art Rust, Jr., sitting in the center-field bleachers at the Stadium, 1939. Hank Greenberg hit a ball on River Avenue, out of the ballpark, but Joseph Paul went between the monuments. But you had it all the time.

DiMaggio: Oh, no, not really! But, yes, I remember that like it was yesterday. And I started to run back, knowing that the ball was hit as hard as it was—and I didn't play him in quite close; I played him pretty deep as it was because he was a powerful hitter. That's how I played guys like him and Jimmy Foxx, those kind of guys. All I did was run with my back to home plate. I was only trying to stop this thing from being a home run. I had to track it down so I could stop him at third base. As I was running, for some reason, I turned and I saw something darting in the air. I threw my gloved hand out . . ."

Rust: And there it was . . .

DiMaggio: And there it was. The ball landed just right . . . in the glove. I'll tell you, I was so surprised and shocked that I tried to shake it out, not knowing that by then it was in my hand.

Rust: Another Art Rust secret memory. It's the '42 World Series and I'm sitting with my Dad in the right-field grandstands, Cardinals and Yankees. It was the Saturday game when White shut you guys out, two to nothing. You hit a line drive to center field. It's Musial's ball, but he slips. Terry Moore grabs it sideways. Do you remember that one?

DiMaggio: I remember it so distinctly. I remember that Series quite well. That is one of the only ones we lost in over ten years; for the last ten years I was in World Series play. Well, what I want to say is that I had seven hits throughout the whole Series. But my long hits were all caught. All I had were singles. It was Enos Slaughter, Moore, or Stan Musial. I hit at least six drives on which they made impossible catches, and that's why that one day that you might have seen me kick the dirt against the Dodgers.

Rust: Al Gionfriddo in the 1947 Series?

DiMaggio: Going to second base . . . that was the result of what happened in that '42 Series. Because I was never as lucky in a World Series.

Rust: But you know something, Joe? If those games where you had hit those long drives had taken place in Sportsman's Park, you'd have had four round-trippers in one game. Am I correct?

DiMaggio: Absolutely right.

Rust: When you hit the ball that Gionfriddo eventually caught, how did you feel?

DiMaggio: I'll tell you something; I'll tell you how I felt. When I hit that ball, I was running as fast as I could. I certainly thought it was out of the ballpark because we had a little breeze going along with it and Gionfriddo was really not playing his right position. He was out of position, and when I got into second base, I heard these people yelling— a tremendous uproar went up, and I thought perhaps it went into the stands. I didn't realize he had made the catch until I saw the ballplayers running off the field. I was really shocked. And that's why I kicked the dirt. It's a good thing I didn't hit the bag because I would have had a broken toe.

Rust: They say that's the only time you showed emotion.

DiMaggio: Yes, I would have to think that was the only time.

Rust: Joe, how about the changes in the game. I mean the game as it is today?

DiMaggio: No doubt, it's a changed game in many respects. The rules are the same, but let's start with number one, the large salaries everyone is getting. In my time, I was one of the highest-paid. I don't envy—I mean, I have nothing against these fellows getting all that kind of money. I think it's just absolutely fantastic. I'm sorry I'm not around to be in on it, see? But, during the time I played, the general managers were very tough to deal with. Just to give you an idea, I think I was a holdout for my first eight years that I played with the Yankees. Trying to get a thousand dollars or fifteen hundred dollars then was like pulling teeth . . .

Rust: His initials are Ed Barrow (Yankees' GM), right?

DiMaggio: Mr. Edward G. Barrow, right.

Rust: Do you feel many ballplayers are overpaid today?

DiMaggio: I don't know about being overpaid, but of course they must have pretty good agents. For their productivity, I must say that some of the fellows are overpaid, certainly. But you know, there are twenty-six teams in baseball today and it's hard to stack up all the good major league ballplayers. There are a smattering of Triple A ballplayers playing in the majors now. Also, the pay is so high in the other sports—like basketball and football. Those prices are escalating and it's taking some fellows who could be good ballplayers away from baseball.

Legends

And there is talk about expansion. I only hope they don't. But other things are different today. The ballparks are different with the grass and Astroturf. We have more baserunners today and there seems to be more speed than there was years ago. From '36 to '51, we didn't steal many bases—we played for the big innings. We had good hitters who could drive the ball. And we kept one of those rallies alive. And it was never over for the Yankees, even with two outs and five runs behind. I can't tell you the records or statistics. But maybe there is a change in the ball, too.

Rust: Joe, there's been a quote which was attributed to you by some writers. Supposedly you told George Steinbrenner that if Dave Winfield was worth so many millions over ten years, then you had to figure that you would be worth much more. Then, the story goes, you said you'd sit down with George and start off by saying, "George, we're about to become partners."

DiMaggio: Well, it wasn't exactly that way. I said, if you're talking about statistics, then I'd have to say I'd be worth more. And I'll tell you that Dave Winfield is a good ballplayer. Don't sell him short. He's good.

Rust: Any others, players in the last ten years or so, that you like to watch play?

DiMaggio: Well, I like to see a complete ballplayer—a fellow like (Fred) Lynn, but unfortunately he gets hurt. I did myself in many years past, but he's the type of ballplayer I like to watch, a fellow who can really run, hit, throw, and field. He hits to all fields, you know. He'd be more productive if he didn't have all those injuries.

Rust: Joe, the advantages—put that in quotes—that Pete Rose had over you . . . he could lay one down. You (the Yankees) didn't bunt. But, when he had that 44-game streak, when he was knocking at your door, he was quoted in the papers the day he was stopped, when he went 0-for-3 or 0-for-4, that the pitcher thought he was throwing in the World Series. You wouldn't have said something like that. Joseph Paul would've said, "Throw me your best shot and let me have a go at it."

DiMaggio: I was quite shocked that Pete made that remark because I know Pete. We went together to entertain the troops in Vietnam and we got to know each other quite well. After all, he surely didn't want the man to put the ball down the middle of the plate so he could hit—that's the challenge of the game. You've got to hit their best pitch. Sometimes we're guess hitters, but everybody is supposed to get their best pitch. I don't think Pete was thinking when he made that remark.

Rust: Joseph, let's go back in time to 1941. I think I saw at least 30 of your hits, your bingles, in that 56-game hitting streak. The night you were stopped, I saw it. I saw it on the radio. Mel Allen did the dramatized recreation of same on Western Union from Cleveland, July 17. It was Jim Bagby and Al Smith. What were you feeling? I remember you hit two screamers to Kenny Keltner, who fielded them like Eddie Giacomin, the hockey goalie. And you also hit a shot to Boudreau at shortstop. Tell me about that.

DiMaggio: You've really got that all down pretty pat. My first time at bat, I believe it was Al Smith who started the game and he walked me on a three-and-two count. He threw me a curveball which broke down in the dirt. So he didn't give me too much to hit. And, naturally, he wanted to stop me like all the rest of them. Second time at bat, I hit a screaming ball down towards left field. Kenny Keltner, who was very graceful, was playing a short left field. That's how far he played. He played right on the line. I had an oppor-

25

tunity to meet him maybe ten years later, and then I asked him, "Kenny, I don't mind the deepness, but why were you playing me down the line?" And he said all he was trying to do was to stop the extra base hit. By gosh, those balls that were hit—you know, he caught them on a half-hop—and he took them in foul territory and he had to make a long throw to first base. Each time the ball got there and my foot got there almost at the same time—just like this, clap-clap! That fast! The second time, I hit an identical shot and he threw me out again.

Now I said if it hadn't rained the night before I possibly would have beaten out those plays because it was too soft running down to first base. It was just one of those things. It got a little muddy but his throwing me out . . . it was like a knock on the door . . . a double knock. And, if it hadn't rained, I think I could've beaten it out, yes.

Rust: Let's backtrack, Joseph. Game 38 of The Streak was in The Bronx. I think you had gone 0-for-3 and Eldon Auker was on the mound for the Browns. Red Rolfe was on first with the shortest lead in history. They had him nailed to first base. Then, with no other at-bats left, you slapped a double to left.

DiMaggio: Well, let me give you more on that. I was fifth in the order and Tommy Heinrich was the next batter. Before going to the plate, he went over and talked to Joe McCarthy. He said, "Joe, we got a lead in this game so why don't I get up there and just sacrifice, because if I hit into a double play it's possible Joe might not be able to get another time at bat." McCarthy said that was a good idea and Tommy did just that. He bunted. So I had my turn at bat and I hit a solid shot over the third baseman's head.

Rust: If I was starting a ballclub, Joseph, I'll tell you my three outfielders—Joseph Paul DiMaggio, Willie Howard

Mays, and Terry Bluford Moore. You guys can play anywhere you want to play. What position do you want?

DiMaggio: Listen, I'd be happy to play in any part of that outfield. I guarantee you I wouldn't be doing much work.

Rust: They always ask me this, my all-star defensive outfield. I say these three guys. Let 'em pick out any spot they want to play.

DiMaggio: You don't have to prove it to me. With that Moore, you know, during the World Series he made some fantastic catches. Willie I didn't get to play with too much. That year, '51, was his first year and my last one.

Rust: Let's discuss your brothers, Vince and Dominic. Vince was no slouch with his glove, either.

DiMaggio: Well, Vince—he was a great outfielder. He played for Pittsburgh and for Cincinnati and he could go out and get 'em. He could hit an awful long ball when he made contact. But he had a blind spot between his letters and his shoulders, and he went right through that ball. He struck out quite a bit. He held the record for a while.

Rust: Why do you suppose Dom made so many great catches off you, Joe?

DiMaggio: Not in Boston, he didn't. He just didn't have enough room there. But, let me give you an old anecdote. I was battling Hank Greenberg for the RBI title with two weeks left to go, or thereabouts, and we had the pennant clinched. We're playing the Red Sox and the first time I came to bat, the bases were loaded. And Dom is out there in center field. I hit a shot out there where that 457-foot sign used to be, before they brought the fences in. And he went as far as he could and he put his hand up against that doggone screen, and you could see half the ball. It wanted to drop out, but he held onto it. That's the third out so I didn't even get an RBI.

So, on the way in, I gave him a flash and looked at him. And, of course, he could read my lips. And he just grinned. He gave me a big smile. When I came up in the seventh inning, the same thing happened. Bases were loaded and I hit another shot out to center field, and he made another one of those catches . . . his back to the plate and it was just fantastic. Well, before the game I had invited him to dinner. So he came to my house and rang the doorbell.

I let him in but I wouldn't talk to him for about three minutes, you know. Finally, he came up with little words of wisdom. "You know, Joe . . ."—words of consolation, I should've said—"I couldn't have gone another inch for either of those balls." It took off the tension, and we laughed and had a good dinner.

Rust: Let's reminisce again. Boston, June, 1949. Arthur George Rust, Jr., graduates from college, and my mother said, "What are you going to do all summer?" I said, "I'm not going to medical school in September. I'll play golf for a while. I want to be a sportscaster." You had missed the first sixty-five games and you came back in Beantown. I took the shuttle. I went up to Boston. My God, three games, four roundtrippers, nine ribbies. Joe, you went nuts!

DiMaggio: I always thought I had missed sixty-seven games. I'm going to take it from you because I've heard so much about your memory. That's when they built that special shoe and I had to get some spring training. The team was in Boston. We had Al Schacht, who pitched batting practice. Remember Al Schacht?

Rust: The clown—sure—the comedian.

DiMaggio: That's correct. And he pitched a little for the Washington Senators. Of course, he's an old-timer. He had a restaurant. In any event, he pitched batting practice to me, and I had three days of working out there at the Stadium. And I decided to go up to Boston because I thought I was just about ready.

Rust: Glad you did.

DiMaggio: I'll never forget Casey Stengel. He was in the clubhouse when I got there, and I was getting dressed and there were about ten newspaper men standing around to find out whether I was going to play or not. My back was to him and he kept looking over at me. And I caught him out of the corner of my eye. He didn't ask me, he just waited for me to say something. I kind of put him on a little bit. You know, I let him wait. Finally, after about five minutes, I thought I would relieve the tension and I gave him a nod, and he said, "All right, gentlemen, here's my lineup."

In any event, I go up there the first time at bat, against this left-hander. I can't recall his name, the Irish boy, and —and he could throw a curve.

Rust: McDermott—Mickey McDermott.

DiMaggio: That's him. He could throw awfully hard. First time I went to bat against him, my gosh, I saw an awful lot of smoke. So, I fouled off about six balls, but they were all on the right side of the field, almost right over their dugout. Finally, I was getting my swing in there and getting to look at all of his fast balls, and I hit one over the shortstop's head for a base hit—a good line drive. And I came up a second time.

Rust: Over Pesky's head?

DiMaggio: Right. And then I hit a home run over the bleachers, and we did very well. We beat them pretty good. And the second game, I got the two home runs. And the third day I batted against, I think it was Lefty Mel Parnell, and I hit one out of the ballpark.

And they were in the thick of the race at that time. But I—I always remember the newspapers belittling the Yankees. They said, "We're waiting for you, and we're gonna get you." They were hot and we were cold.

Rust: That reminds me of the night you almost became a Red Sox.

DiMaggio: I think I know the story.

Rust: First, let me tell you it took place at Toots Shor's. That's where the drinking fiasco, with Tom Yawkey and Dan Topping, started. Am I historically accurate?

DiMaggio: This was . . . you know, I was in the twilight of my career, and they had talked about making the change and wanting to see what the difference might be . . . maybe the year or two I had left with Ted (Williams) being at the Stadium and hitting in that short porch. I mean, compared to where he was hitting and vice-versa with me. They went along and they just about shook hands on the deal, and the following day when they woke up they couldn't reach each other fast enough to say, "What did we do?" And, you know, they talked themselves out of that one.

Rust: Joe, that brings up a question people often ask me. Why didn't you stay in baseball, in some capacity?

DiMaggio: I really did want to stay in baseball. I was with the Oakland ballclub when they first came to Oakland. I was with them in 1967 as a coach. I was really hired to do front-office work but I wound up on the field. I was with them for three years, and the reason I did get out was because of the fact that I did have a bad stomach, and it was very difficult to find the right time to eat. We were playing night baseball and day baseball. It was bothering me. But I

Joe DiMaggio

was looking forward to being in baseball, and at that time the commissioner offered me a job out there to be his liaison man on the West Coast. His offer to me, though, was such a peoned piece of change that I decided I'd better stay out of it. I'd better try to make a living on the outside.

Rust: Another incident people often mention was the '39 Series when Keller hit Lombardi in Cincinnati. Do you recall it?

DiMaggio: I'll tell you there was a man on third and first and I got the base hit between first and second to right field. Ival Goodman, who was playing right field, fielded the ball and threw to third base, and I guess it got by there. I don't remember it too clearly, but I do remember . . .

Rust: Billy Werber?

DiMaggio: Werber, yes—but in going around second I could see what was happening. I was going into third base and Art Fletcher, our coach, was trying to hold me up at third base because what had happened was that Charlie Keller had hit Lombardi on the side of the head. And he was safe, naturally, and the ball just stood—it was right by home plate. He was laying there prone and Fletcher was trying to hold me up and I'm going around, and he just practically lassoed me and I went through. But Ernie Lombardi woke up, picked up the ball, and put it in front of home plate, and for some reason I made one of those hook slides and I was right over his glove. I was right over his hand and I touched the outer part of the plate. Now Babe Pinelli, who lives in California and is still around, called that safe. He called it the way he saw it. Bucky Walters kept arguing with Pinelli, but Pinelli really did call the right play.

Rust: How about your rookie year, Joe? What stood out?

Legends

DiMaggio: My first year, 1936? I tell you—I was only a kid, you know, and I'd dreamed about being in a World Series when I was a youngster playing a little softball around the North Beach Playground in San Francisco . . . and to get to the major leagues and join the New York Yankees, and to play in the World Series and to win the championship. I realized that my very first year. My boyhood dream came true within my first year.

Rust: Let's go back a little further, to 1932, the Pacific Coast League, and the opportunity you got with the San Francisco Seals.

DiMaggio: It was the last three games of the season. Augie Galan was playing shortstop and Prince Henry Oana, who was a Hawaiian, was out there in left field. And they were stuck in sixth place, not going down and not going up.

Oana had an opportunity to play some exhibition games and the Seals let him go. He requested to have Augie Galan go with him. On that basis, they were left without a shortstop. My brother, Vince, who had just joined the San Francisco ballclub, made a recommendation. He said, "Well, I got a brother to play shortstop." And they said, "We heard about your brother. We've got a scouting system, too." That was Charlie Graham, owner of the ballclub.

Naturally, I was a little nervous, but not all that nervous because I wasn't cocky in that sense. But I just felt I had enough confidence that I could play baseball in the Pacific Coast League. But they put me at shortstop. Here was my problem. Whenever I fielded the ball, I always threw it some place in the stands. And I could throw awfully hard. Of course, the second day I was there, I played shortstop— why, they let a whole section be clear. And they used the expression, "He's got it again." And, by gosh, if I wouldn't break one of those seats throwing over the first baseman's head, you know, into the stands. My first time at bat—I do remember the fellow's name; it was Ted Pillette—and I hit a triple to right center field and that started me in baseball.

Rust: A cliche question, Joe, but how about your toughest pitchers?

DiMaggio: Yes, I'll name one who was my nemesis of all time, the toughest pitcher I ever faced. That was Mel Harder of the Cleveland Indians. He threw an assortment—a little sinker and a curveball which was, perhaps, the greatest curveball in the American League, along with Tommy Bridges of Detroit. He would move the ball around and I had a difficult time in hitting him.

Rust: Got to ask you, Joseph, about another Indian, one Robert Feller?

DiMaggio: Well, Bobby Feller—I was very, very lucky— I mean, through the years I played he could certainly throw hard and he had a great curveball because Mel Harder taught Bobby that curveball. Although Bobby would show me the curve, he would never let me hit it. I would hit his fastball. And I hit the man. I should never have deserved to hit that man as good as I did.

Rust: Surely you recall April 30, 1946, when he no-hit the Yankees?

DiMaggio: Of course, he was pretty fast. He had great control that day as I remember. In the bottom of the ninth, it was Henrich, myself, and Keller. I think Tommy Henrich hit one of those balls down to first base. And Les Fleming, I think, fumbled it. He was trying to pick it up, you know, he didn't want that thing to take a bad hop and he fumbled it. Well, finally, Henrich got on base, and so it was like getting four outs. You know, when you're pitching a no-hitter game, why, three is enough. So that was actually another out.

Legends

Rust: When many people talk about the three greatest ball-players, the same names keep cropping up. Often you hear Joseph Paul, Willie Mays, and Mickey Mantle. How about that threesome?

DiMaggio: Thanks for putting me in there. That's great company. You can't go wrong in picking those other gentlemen, and why you picked me I don't know because, listen, we have fellows like in the other league . . . Stan Musial certainly was a great ballplayer. Ted Williams had some problems, maybe, out on the field and he looked a little awkward running, but certainly he could do all the offensive things.

Rust: Those are two great hitters, but you were three great ballplayers.

DiMaggio: Okay, you're talking about competition— well, that's very nice, but I'll tell you Ted was about the best hitter ever in the game of baseball. You know, I didn't get to see Lou Gehrig, and I saw Jimmy Foxx, Hank Greenberg, and Rudy York. But I caught those gentlemen at the tail end of their careers. I would still have to say that Ted was naturally among the best.

Rust: Mel Allen once kept track of all your long outs at the Stadium, Joseph, trying to figure out how many home runs you'd have hit in a ballpark with human dimensions.

DiMaggio: I did hit quite a few shots at the Stadium that were flagged down. Not even great catches but, at 440 feet, they were waiting for the ball to come down, to pick it off. Just like I did many times against Greenberg, Jimmy Foxx, and a fellow named Bob Johnson . . . and Rudy York . . . they were all such tremendous hitters. In the alley, they couldn't get that base hit.

Joe DiMaggio

Rust: You mentioned Lou Gehrig. You did see him at the very end. It was April 30, 1939, and after Mass I told my father I wanted to go to the ballpark. You guys were playing the Washington Senators—Lou's last game. What are your memories of Gehrig?

DiMaggio: Was that the last game he played? Well, I do remember he took himself out. McCarthy wouldn't take him out. He said, "Joe, I think my streak has come to an end." Joe McCarthy took him out at Lou's request. Let me give you a description of Lou as I saw him. He couldn't run too good. He looked a little awkward but, by gosh, nobody played harder than he did. When he went from first to third, you saw him running—he had an odd kind of gait, you know. Well, he just shook all over, but he always managed to get there or close to it, and he . . . he was a strange man. He thought he had to produce in every game to be a winner. In other words, if he went 0-for-4 or 0-for-5, or if he had a bad day on the field, he would blame himself. And he would take the responsibility of why we lost that day and he would sulk in the clubhouse. He was a team man 100 percent and he was a fine gentleman.

Rust: Another incident which always comes up. The '41 Series and the Mickey Owen dropped strike. That had to be one of the strangest things that ever happened.

DiMaggio: You know what happened the next day when Tommy Henrich had the two strikes. It was Casey that was pitching and, of course, Owen takes the blame for it as a passed ball. I don't know if he knew that the ball was loaded. Later on he did know that it was loaded because he had never thrown a pitch like that—and I was the next batter and I never saw a pitch like that. That one broke down and, of course, it took him by surprise and hit the end of that glove of his and went to the stands. We found out later on it was a loaded-up ball.

Rust: In 1938, Joseph, you hit .381, but you were going at a .412 clip with two weeks left and then you had an eye infection. You told McCarthy you really couldn't see the ball.

DiMaggio: Actually, I had a cold in the eye. I still don't know what they analyzed it as but I had to take a shot of cocaine so that I could open my eye. And it was the lead eye because, as a right-handed hitter, it was my left eye that was bothering me.

I was hitting .412 with two weeks left to play. And we already had the pennant cinched as well. But he made one comment to me. He said, "Joe, you probably are thinking as to why I'm making you play or why I got you in the lineup. I don't want you to be a 'cheese champion.' " I went along with that. I played. But I lost thirty-two points in two weeks.

Rust: A continuing debate but not really a debate, Joseph. How about Phil Rizzuto not being in Cooperstown?"

DiMaggio: I played behind him for many, many years and I'll tell you that man never made a mistake. He came out for a relay. He was in the right spot at all times. And he could hit that ball, he could get on base. He could do so many things. He could bunt, hit, and run. He was a very valuable man. I think one day he will be in there.

Rust: Joe, what are you doing these days? Just briefly?

DiMaggio: Well, I'm still with the Bowery Bank and will be discussing contract with Mr. Coffee. Of course, I've been playing a little golf, usually for charity events, you know.

Rust: You know what my handicap is?

Joe DiMaggio

DiMaggio: No.

Rust: Just going out on the course. Joe, well, God bless you. Thank you. It's a thrill. From 1936 to 1951, nobody did it like you did.

DiMaggio: Thanks.

3

Bob
Feller

YOU *say Bob Feller to me
and I think about him striking out eighteen Detroit Tigers
in the last game of the 1938 season. And I recall that he
stopped Hank Greenberg's chances of catching Babe Ruth's
sixty home-run record. Greenberg went into the last-day
doubleheader needing two homers, and he was stopped
cold. I also remember Feller striking out Detroit's Chet
Laabs five times.*

*I was at Yankee Stadium on Opening Day in 1946
when Feller, fresh out of the service, no-hit the Yankees,
1-0. His battery-mate, Frankie Hayes, hit the game-winning
round-tripper off righty Bill Bevens. A high-kicking Feller
struck out 11 Yankees that day.*

*What's Feller like off the field? He's honest in his eval-
uations of ballplayers. He shoots straight from the shoulder, a
trait that hasn't endeared him to some people. He once said
Jackie Robinson was just another muscle-bound football
player. But he was pleasantly surprised by Jackie's success.*

Rust: Bob, let's go back to how Bob Feller was discovered.
I remember Cy Slapnicka, who was a Cleveland scout, went

west to scout a pitcher I saw with the Phillies and the Chicago Cubs by the name of Claude Passeau. How did he stumble over you?

Feller: I pitched in American Legion ball around Des Moines, Iowa, and he had been told by the umpires that I had a pretty good arm. So one day, the following year, after I was out of American Legion ball, and I was playing professionally in semi-pro ball in Des Moines, he came out to see Claude Passeau. Passeau was with the Des Moines Demons, and Cy had the intention to buy him for the Cleveland ballclub. He came to see me pitch that morning and the next. It was a tournament game, and he never did go to see Claude Passeau. He stayed there and watched me pitch. He talked to my dad and mother, but I didn't sign that day, I signed about a week or 10 days later, and, of course, I went to Cleveland and Passeau went to the National League. And Slapnicka, who was living in Cedar Rapids, scouted and signed fellows like Bill Zuber, who pitched for the Yankees and the Indians and other clubs. He signed Lou Boudreau and Kenny Keltner, Hal Trosky, and on and on and on. Mel Harder was one of his men, and he brought up a lot of players. He signed by far more ball players, and good ones, than anybody else in the Cleveland organization.

Slapnicka was their chief scout. He became general manager that year, after he signed me in the fall of 1935, and I came to Cleveland in '36 after my junior year in high school. I pitched sandlot ball here. I was supposed to go to Fargo, North Dakota, but I did very well in an exhibition game against the Cardinals. My arm was a little tired, pitching in the state tournament in Iowa, and I told him about it. There was nothing wrong. I pitched against the Cardinals and I struck out eight of nine of the Gas House gang, with Joe Medwick and Pepper Martin and the Dean boys, Dizzy and Paul, Frankie Frisch, and Rip Collins and Leo Durocher and many more. In fact, Durocher was my first strikeout. I think I got him twice in those three innings, because I walked a few and they got a couple of hits, and they scored one run.

Rust: Now listen, didn't Rickey try to sign you—Branch Rickey, for the Cardinals?

Feller: Ah, yes, but my father was not too interested in any ballclub but Cleveland. He didn't care that much for the Cardinals chain-gang operation. They weren't paying you very much money. That's why eventually some jumped down to Mexico after World War Two.

Rust: There were cries of illegality about your contract with the Indians, and the late Judge Kenesaw Mountain Landis had to intervene. Tell me about that.

Feller: Well, Art, in those days the way they helped finance the minor leagues . . . the major league clubs did what they were supposed to do. Each minor league team had territorial rights to a certain area within a certain distance of their ballpark or their home city. And they had a right to sign all the players within that region. But the major league clubs were cheating and signing them directly with the ballclub and making underhand deals with the minor league ballclubs to hide the players and let them play for them as if they had signed them. Of course, they threw that out in the fall of 1936 at the major league meeting, but Judge Landis didn't want to give me my release like he did release a lot of players.

Rust: The Cards lost Pete Reiser, among others.

Feller: How's that?

Rust: Pete Reiser was one of them.

Feller: Yes. It could be. There were about 190 or so of them released. Benny McCoy was the player . . .

Rust: Benny McCoy, with the Philadelphia Athletics.

Feller: Yes. He went to Philadelphia. I guess he got around $45 or $50 thousand—it was a lot of bucks in those days but . . .

Rust: And an automobile.

Feller: Could be. I know I had scouts from Boston and New York around Des Moines, and there at the Chamberlain Hotel they had blank checks. I could have picked up a quarter of a million, but my dad wanted me to stay with Cleveland. They fined the Cleveland ballclub $7,500 and let me remain with the Cleveland Indians.

Rust: Bob, your first start—against the St. Louis Browns —you struck out . . . you had fifteen *K*s that day. Tell me about it.

Feller: Well, I had pretty good control that day. I wasn't as wild as I was a lot of times. I had fifteen strike-outs. When I started to warm up to pitch in the game, they had Denny Galehouse warming up in the bullpen. And every time I walked to the mound, at the end of every inning, Denny would get up and loosen up again. He continued to throw in the bullpen until about—oh, past the middle of the game, maybe the sixth or seventh inning, and he would warm up every time I warmed up at the start of every inning. Finally, in the last couple or three innings, why, Denny did not get up any more, and I just went ahead and finished the ballgame. It was in the middle of August. It was the twenty-third of August, to be a fact, because this was my fiftieth anniversary with the Indians. They had quite a little celebration commemorating my fiftieth anniversary in the city of Cleveland with the Indians. Of course, I never did go to another ballclub. I am still with the Indians and have been for eight years, and looking forward, of course, to going to Spring training and helping coach the big club as well as some of the papooses in the farm system. I got to the majors when I was seventeen. I was the youngest pitcher to ever start a game, ever to win a game, and ever to complete a game, even during World War Two when most able-bodied men were out fighting the war. In 1944, they had Joe Nuxhall of the Cincinnati Reds. Of course he was too young for military service—he was fifteen. Carl Scheib was sixteen. They both did pitch in a ballgame, but one of them pitched only one inning. Scheib pitched one inning, and Nuxhall pitched two-thirds of an inning. Neither one of them started again for some time. It was about six years. I think Scheib was nineteen when he started his first game.

Rust: You know, what stands out in my mind, and I remember this quite clearly, was the last day of the 1938 season against the Tigers. You struck out eighteen guys. You got Chet Laabs five times. Hank Greenberg needed two round-trippers to tie Babe Ruth. I think you struck him out a couple of times that day.

Feller: I think I got Hank twice that day. I know that it was a double-header and Hank needed two home runs to tie Ruth and three to beat him. Those were the days before they had the fence on the inside of Cleveland Stadium, and unless you pulled the ball. . . .

Rust: That was League Park, right?

Feller: That was in—no, it was Municipal Stadium. We played at League Park. We played there through '46. However, on weekends, we played at the Municipal Stadium— the games that we thought were going to attract a lot of people, because League Park only seated 23,000. So, they would move the tarpaulin. They'd move all our uniforms

Bob Feller

and stuff down to Municipal Stadium where they are playing now. When Bill Veeck got there in 1946, we played in League Park, and he made a deal with the city. He turned the ballpark over to the city for whatever amount of money he got out of it—or concessions or rent. That was the end of the League Park.

Rust: I was in junior high school when you pitched that no-hitter opening day of 1940. I believe it was in Comiskey Park. I believe you beat Ted Lyons. Am I correct?

Feller: No, it was against Edgar Smith.

Rust: Oh, Ed Smith—Ed Smith, the left-hander. All right.

Feller: He had beaten me some ballgames but I beat him in that one. Of course, I did pitch against Ted Lyons many, many times, and Ted was the guy that started 20 games one year, and he finished all 20, all on Sundays. That was at the end of his career. He was a pretty good hitter, too, for a pitcher, and I knew Ted well. He passed away in 1987, down in Louisiana. I had talked to him just about two or three weeks before he passed away. He was very weak, but he was a great guy. But Ed Smith, the left-hander, pitched against me in that game in Chicago. We won it 1-0 when my catcher, Hemsley—Rollie Hemsley—tripled my roommate, Jeff Heath, across the plate after he had singled.

Rust: Rollicking Rollie Hemsley.

Feller: Rollicking Rollie was a fine catcher; I liked Rollie. He was a good fastball catcher, and he would call for a lot of fastballs.

Rust: That's what you had, Bob!

Feller: I had a fastball and Frankie Pytlak . . . he was with us too, and he would . . . he would call for a curveball. He caught me the day I struck out eighteen, and I bought him

43

a suit of clothes for that little effort. Frankie was a very good friend of mine. Frankie and Rollie were excellent catchers. Both of them were good hitters, too.

Rust: I was at your no-hitter in 1946 at the Stadium when Frankie Hayes hit that home run.

Feller: All my catchers have passed away . . . Jim Hegan, Frankie Hayes, Hemsley, and Pytlak. All four of them are now gone. Lollar, too. I pitched under Sherman Lollar too —not that much, of course.

Rust: Don't forget Billy Sullivan.

Feller: Billy Sullivan. I pitched a little under Billy Sullivan. He's still living in Florida, around the Sarasota area. But he didn't catch me that much. Billy was a good hitter, not that great a defensive man. But he was an excellent hitter, and he could bunt and drag. He went to St. Louis, too. In fact, he got a bunt. He drug one one day in Cleveland with the Browns. That was the only hit of the ballgame. It was my first one-hitter, as a matter of fact. I had a lot of catchers here, and of course some caught more than others. In the service I had a lot of different catchers. I pitched to Walker Cooper at Great Lakes in '45, and Vinnie Smith, who caught for the Pirates, in '42 down in Norfolk. I was only in Norfolk a short time, and then I went aboard the battleship *Alabama* and went to Europe. From there I went to the South Pacific for a little over two years. When I returned from sea duty, which was almost a three-year stint, I took over Mickey Cochrane's place at Great Lakes. There were some pretty good ballplayers, like Denny Galehouse, Pinky Higgins, Kenny Keltner. We found Johnny Groth there; he was just an eighteen-year-old kid out of a Catholic school in Chicago.

Rust: With the Detroit Tigers?

Feller: Yes. And, we had many other players that played major league ball—Tommy Upton of the Browns, Ed Carnett of the White Sox.

Rust: When you came up in '36 Lou Gehrig was around, Lucius Appling was around, Joseph Paul's first year, DiMaggio that is, Ted "the thumper" in '39, Tommy Henrich, Al Simmons, Foxx, Hank Greenberg—who were the toughest hitters for Bobby Feller?

Feller: I have to give DiMaggio that because Joe was the toughest hitter for me as a right-hand hitter. He was not the toughest overall, but he was by far the toughest right-hand hitter for me. I didn't get Joe out much until about the last three years he was in the league, '49, '50, and '51. And New York Yankee Henrich was probably the other toughest hitter for me, followed very closely by Taft Wright, who played for the Chicago White Sox. Stan Spence, then with the Washington Senators; Roy Cullenbine, then with St. Louis Browns; the Boston Red Sox Johnny Pesky; and Nellie Fox, and Rip Radcliff with the Chicago White Sox.

Rust: What made them tough? These are contact guys you are talking about?

Feller: Mostly things were my own fault, because I continued to throw fastballs. I was hard-headed enough not to throw them curves or change-ups or sliders. I continued to throw them fastballs, thinking I could throw 'em by them, and those fellows were tough. I knew Tommy Henrich wasn't a good curveball hitter, but I kept trying to throw fastballs by him, and he kept hitting them by my ear and out of the ballpark or for base hits. Tommy wasn't all that much of a home run hitter, but he did have a lot of power.

Rust: All right. Your one and only World Series start in '48 against the Boston Braves ballclub. Johnny Sain bested you, as we say in a journalistic way.

Legends

Feller: Well, I did start in two games. I got my brains beaten out in Cleveland in the fifth game, but we won the Series, and then two days later it was in Boston. We won it in the sixth, and I combined with Bob Lemon. I had the start and Lemon relieved me, and we won it in Boston. My first one, Art, was in Boston. . . .

Rust: Phil Masi.

Feller: A two-hitter. Sain beat me. Tommy Holmes got a hit after we thought we had two out. We picked Phil Masi off second by about three feet. He ran for Bill Salkeld, who I had walked to start the inning, and that's another lesson for you. Never walk the leadoff man. He had fouled off about a half-dozen pitches, and finally I missed the plate with one of them and he got a base on balls. Then the pinch runner went in. He was sacrificed, and then the pitcher, Johnny Sain, popped up. Tommy Holmes came up and got a single after we tried the pick-off play. And I thought we had Masi picked off by a couple of feet, which everybody else did, too. That was the first year that the World Series was televised coast to coast.

Rust: All right now. You didn't get a chance in '54 when the Indians played the New York Giants. What were your feelings that year?

Feller: We had a good ballclub that year. We had a lot of good pitchers to start—Bob Lemon, Early Wynn, Mike Garcia, Art Houtteman, Ray Narleski, and Don Mossi. And I went 13-and-3 that year. Wynn and Lemon had twenty or more wins and Mike Garcia won nineteen. Houtteman had fifteen. Lemon pitched with two days rest. And that is one of the only Series that I know of that was played—for whatever reason—without any time out for travel. We played four straight, right on through, Wednesday through Saturday.

And, of course, they beat us four straight. Lemon

pitched a good game the first game, and then he got beat in ten innings by Dusty Rhodes' home run with two on—about a 257-footer right down the right-field line in the Polo Grounds. And then Wynn pitched a good game the next day, and Rhodes pinch-hit again and he hit one up on the roof. He hit that ball real good. He didn't hit the first one off Lemon good at all. And then back in Cleveland, Garcia lost, and we were in a batting slump. We didn't look that good. Not all of our hitters were in a slump, though. Vic Wertz was not in a slump. He hit .500 and he hit the ball that Willie Mays caught way out there by the fence in the bleachers. Willie made that very fine catch. It would have been the ballgame if he hadn't caught up with it.

Rust: What about the night that you struck out—I forgot whether it was eight, nine, or ten, and then you fell off the mound and injured yourself?

Feller: That was in '47, Art. I struck out, oh, I think it was all but one man in the first four innings, and then I slipped on the mound on the last pitch with two strikes to Hank Majeski of the Philadelphia Athletics. It was a curveball. I slipped because of loose dirt. It was my own fault. I did not knock down the dirt where I stepped when I would pivot on my pivot foot out in front. I usually kept straightening it away, because I stepped off a little differently, I think, on the curveball. On the fastball you grapple up a little loose dirt. Most fellows step a little differently on the curve. They open up their body a little more. Your step is a little bit shorter, and I step a little more to the left, being a right-handed pitcher, and that's what caused me to fall. And I missed the All-Star Game in Chicago. The fellow that took my place that year was a winning pitcher, Frank "Spec" Shea.

Rust: When you had that high kick toward third base, did that throw you off any?

Legends

Feller: I had good balance. Of course, it took me a couple of years to learn how, with men on base, to keep that front foot down and my body back and to shove off with the back leg. That, mixed with the pump-handled wind-up, the short pump-handle, the big one . . . I liked the big wind-up. Now they don't take the wind-up like they used to. I think that you speed it up or slow it down. It does assist you almost as much as another good pitch in your repertoire. I was just naturally wild, and I was very careless, because I could throw all day and never get tired.

Rust: All right, Bobby, you had a feud—yes or no?—with Jack Roosevelt Robinson? Yes or no?

Feller: Well, not really a feud. I'm writing a book right now, and this is, of course, one of the parts of the book. I wouldn't call it a feud. I was never mad at Jackie for any particular reason. I think that Jackie was . . . oh, he was a real competitor. We both went into the Hall of Fame in Cooperstown, and we were standing there side by side, along with Bill McKechnie and Eddie Roush, over here from Indiana.

Rust: I think you predicted, if my mind serves me correctly, that Jackie would never make the big leagues.

Feller: I think I said that because he looked like another muscle-bound football player. It was more or less a tongue-in-cheek thing. We were playing exhibition games in California against each other and—you know, it's like Bill Veeck always said—if you've got a feud going, don't keep it a secret. This was more or less of a little hype to help our exhibition games. Jackie was a great athlete. He never did really hit the high, tight fastball very good. I could throw a pretty good high, tight fastball in my prime, and maybe I didn't take it into consideration . . . that not too many guys were hitting it if I got it where I wanted it. I don't know if

Bob Feller

I ever said that Jackie wasn't going to make the big leagues—that he wasn't a good ballplayer. It was more or less in jest or to hype up our exhibition games, which we were playing on the West Coast.

Rust: I tell you what I do remember, though, Bob. You were among the first, if not actually the very first Numero Uno, to go to bat for Satchel Paige for his election into the Hall of Fame.

Feller: Satchel was always a good friend of mine. As a matter of fact, while we are talking about this—they have a Negro old-timers' reunion down in Ashville, Kentucky . . .

Rust: It was about two years ago.

Feller: I'm the only white ballplayer they invited. And the reason they did is because I played against the black ball-players just before World War II, starting back in '36. We played them after the war. We played them all over the United States. And they say that I helped the American public see the greatness of the black ballplayers in competing against the best ballplayers in the American and National League, which I had my team made up of. That told the club owners something . . . that they could compete. Furthermore, it also showed the great drawing power of the West Coast. We played in San Francisco, San Diego, Oakland, Los Angeles—both Gilmore Field and old Wrigley Field. We played up and down California after about the middle of the month. In the meantime, we played in major league ballparks back east, like Yankee Stadium. We played against Satchel Paige on a Friday and on a Sunday down there in Yankee Stadium. With the two ballgames together we drew over a hundred thousand people at major league prices. This was right around the World Series in 1946. So as far as Jackie goes, I was glad to see him in the Hall of Fame. He was a great athlete. He belonged in the big leagues, and I know people predicted that Carl Hubbell couldn't win in the big leagues, too. I'm not a baseball scout, but what I said was that I was not oblivious to the fact that a little razzamatazz in the newspapers might put a few more people in the seats, and it did.

Rust: How did Satchel take the fact that blacks couldn't play in major league baseball at the time that you guys were barnstorming together?

Feller: Well, there was nothing he ever said about it. It was just the way it was. It was understood—which was, of course, not the way we wanted it. I wouldn't have had my Bob Feller All-Stars playing coast-to-coast after the war or even before the war. We had our own airplanes after the war and we traveled by car and plane before. You can't saw sawdust—what's been done has been done. Sometimes good health and a short memory is not all bad. The facts are there and it wasn't right, but it's been taken care of. Not as soon as it should have been, but nothing was ever said about him not playing major league ball. We were in this thing to give a lot of good entertainment and to give the fans a chance to see the whites against the blacks—it was a racial rivalry trip. We all made a lot of money, and they understood that. I was running the show along with the Kansas City Monarch people, but I was the one that made the deal. We knew that we had a good thing going, and everybody smiled all the way to the bank. And that was all there was to it. Nothing more, nothing less.

Rust: You walked a lot of people. You struck out a lot of people. You threw, therefore, an enormous amount of pitches. You had four years out for the war. If you had pitched those four major league seasons, do you think that with all the wear and tear on your arm you could have pitched up until as long as you did?

Bob Feller

Feller: I have heard that question before. I am not a believer that you only have so many pitches in your arm. I think I am a believer in the way you take care of yourself and recover. If you can't recover with three days rest, you might not recover with a month's rest. I don't believe in this five-day rotation, and I don't believe in counting pitches, and I never did. I believe that you throw when you feel good, and if you're not smart enough to know how much to throw, or when you have had enough, you're not very bright.

And I think a lot of these things came up with kids in Little Leagues. They start telling them that, and it continues right on through their baseball careers in the majors too. You got some guy there with a counter, making marks in the sand or on a piece of paper. I think you can tell how you feel. Some days you feel different than others. Would I have lasted a little longer? Not a bit. I believe that you can play ball the year 'round, with the proper conditioning and getting your rest and doing your exercise. Nobody ever developed a muscle by resting it, did they?

Sure, there is wear and tear, but I played in the South Pacific when we went into port about a couple or three days every month as we were island hopping. I was in the Third Fleet—helping MacArthur do what he said he was going to do, return to Tokyo Bay, and he did. I think that all those four years did for me was to keep me from winning another 100 ballgames.

Rust: Bobby, I remember talking to Dick Bartell out in Chicago about three years ago at the time when I met you at the All-Star game. And Bartell has always convinced me . . . he tries to convince everybody that Van Lingle Mungo threw harder than you did. What's your thought on that?

Feller: That's a funny thing about Bartell. First time I pitched against Bartell was in spring training against the

Giants, and I guess it was in either Pittsburgh or New Orleans. We were training in New Orleans. And Bartell grounded out that day. He came back to the Giants' bench and he said, "Ah, that kid hasn't got a darn thing. There are ten guys in our league who can throw harder than he can." And he named them. After that, Bartell came to bat nineteen times and he struck out sixteen times. It got to be such a joke that the Giant players couldn't wait to see Bartell come to bat against me. They would be rolling on the bench, laughing, slapping each other on the back, on the knees. Both clubs were laughing like heck at Dick Bartell every time he would come back after striking out, and he's saying "That kid hasn't got anything."

Rust: What are you doing these days? Are you doing a lot of hunting or what?

Feller: Oh, I just did this hunting thing one day with the governor . . . it was a homecoming for an Iowan. As a matter of fact, one of the guys from Iowa was Paul Tibbetts. He was the fellow who flew the B-29—you know, that dropped the bomb on Hiroshima. A lot of us Iowans were back there. We got a few birds and had a lot of fun. I work for the Indians. I do P.R. I coach in spring training in Tucson. I work for the major league club, plus the papooses—the farm system, and do a lot of rubber-chicken circuit, knife-and-fork league all around. I help promote the Cleveland Indians. We've got a good ballclub. We're gonna be better next year.

4

Stan Musial

THE first time I saw Stan Musial was at the Polo Grounds. He was with the St. Louis Cardinals. It was September of '41, the final month of the season. And Stan was fresh up from the Rochester Red Wings of the International League. He came up with third baseman Whitey Kurowski and outfielder Erv Dusak. As a thirteen-year-old, I cornered and introduced myself to Musial outside the ballpark.

I found him to be a decent, intelligent person with a kind of laid-back drive. I accompanied Musial that fall day down the subway steps, through the turnstile and into the subway car. I rode all the way with him on the "A" train to the hotel the team was staying at in midtown. He seemed pleased and responsive towards this kid who knew so much about him, having read reams of copy on him in The Sporting News. I will always love Musial for that bit of serendipity, brief though it was.

What really struck me about him was that peculiar batting stance of his. It was like a disco dancer getting in rhythm before the onslaught of the dance floor.

Legends

Rust: Stan, let me tell you something, I saw you at the Polo Grounds in September, 1941—you, Whitey Kurowski, Erv Dusak, fresh up from the Rochester Red Wings of the International League. What were your thoughts that September when you came up and played twelve games and the Cardinals were still pursuing the Dodgers? Was it to try to win the pennant?

Musial: Well, that's right. We were in the thick of the pennant race back then in 1941. When I joined the Cardinals, Billy Southworth put me in the lineup very quickly and I got started great. And I got some hits. I got about two hits a game. I had a phenomenal three weeks at the end there. It was a pleasant surprise, because I started out in Class C that year and I jumped up to the majors, so that was a big thrill for me.

Rust: All right, now name some of the other guys that were on the ballclub that year, as if I didn't know.

Musial: Well, of course, you know, we had Jimmy Brown and Terry Moore and Enos Slaughter and Marty Marion and Walker Cooper and Mort Cooper and Max Lanier. We just had a great all-around club. Really, it was a great ballclub.

Rust: Now, how did baseball start for Stan Musial from Donora, Pennsylvania? How did it all come about?

Musial: Actually, I started playing American Legion baseball for a year, and of course I had played a lot of little pickup games more or less, and then we had a high school team for the first time in my high school. I was an outstanding player and a pitcher at that time, and I hit fourth. And that's how the Cardinals saw me, in high school baseball, but I played in a semi-pro league with the guys who were twenty or twenty-one, and I was only about sixteen. That was a great experience before I played that one year in high school.

Stan Musial

Rust: Who were your idols when you were a youngster?

Musial: Well, you know I had a couple of idols when I was young, being that I was born and raised near Pittsburgh, in Donora, which is about thirty-five miles south of Pittsburgh. I used to root for Paul Waner. I used to watch his averages, watch to see how he was doing. The other fellow I watched—because I was a pitcher, and he was my idol—was Carl Hubbell of the New York Giants. So I had two idols and I watched both of these fellows when I was young. Of course, as years went on, I got to play against both of them. That was really a big thrill.

Rust: All right. Now I understand that you had a tryout with the Pittsburgh Pirates, under Pie Traynor.

Musial: Well, believe it or not, I did. It was a very unusual circumstance. Back in '37 when the Cardinals signed me, I was going to get out of school around June 1st, and the Cardinals were going to tell me where to report. I didn't hear from the Cardinals for about two weeks after school was out in June. So a friend of mine knew Pie Traynor, the manager of the Pittsburgh Pirates. He took me down there, and I was working out with the Pirates for a couple of days. I was throwing batting practice and Traynor liked me. He told me to come back and throw again in batting practice. All of a sudden, about the middle of June, I got this telegram from the Cardinals telling me to report to their club down in Williamson, West Virginia, the Class B club.

Rust: That was in 1938, right?

Musial: That's right. After I got this telegram, I went in and I told Pie Traynor what had happened, and he wanted to know if my father had signed the contract with the Cardinals. I said, yes, my dad did sign because I was underage and he had to sign for me, although he didn't want to. Pie

55

Legends

Traynor told me, "Son, if you ever come back . . . if you're ever out of a job, come back and see the Pirates again."

Rust: Didn't the Yankees and Indians invite you to come in for tryouts?

Musial: Yes, indeed. One of my high school basketball coaches knew the New York Yankee scouts, and they invited me to come out. But it seemed like the Cardinals were the first ones who approached me directly, and I was anxious to start playing baseball. That's why I signed with the Cardinals.

Rust: If my memory serves me correctly, you came up with Dusak and Kurowski, but I think Branch Rickey had his mind set on Erv Dusak. He was a big guy, who had a helluva lot of right-handed power.

Musial: When Dusak and I came up, he had better credentials than I did. He could hit for power, and he had a strong arm. I was surprised at the Cardinals when Southworth put me right in the lineup, but they were very high on Erv Dusak. As time went on, they found around the league—going around the league a few times—that Dusak had trouble hitting the curveball. So he never did come around as well as I did.

Rust: I am going to tell you something that will throw you—this is right off the top of my head. I can tell you the first pitcher you ever went up against. Who was that?

Musial: The first pitcher?

Rust: Yeah. The first major league pitcher you ever went up against.

Musial: Oh, I remember that very well, Art, because . . . it was Jim Tobin of the Boston Braves.

Stan Musial

Rust: Yes, that's right . . . of the Boston Bees then, Stanley.

Musial: Oh, the Boston Bees then, yes, that's right. I remember this distinctly because when I first got up to the plate, this guy was throwing me pitches up. I never did see them in the minor leagues. The ball was floating up and jumping around, you know.

Rust: An old knuckleball.

Musial: I never saw anything like that. So, sure enough, the first time up I popped up to third. A couple of innings later I came up with a couple of men on and I doubled against the screen in right field, and then I got another hit, so I was on my way.

Rust: You started off as a left-handed pitcher. Of course, that's what you are. And you hurt your shoulder. You actually played in the outfield and pitched. Elaborate on that for me.

Musial: I was playing down in Class D ball, down in Daytona Beach, Florida. Once in a while I would play the outfield when I wasn't pitching, and in fact, I played in the outfield for three days and I pitched on the fourth. One day late in the season, back in '40, I guess it was, I was out in center field . . . I was coming in on a shoestring catch and I was going to tumble over and catch the ball. I didn't tumble over. My shoulder jarred as it hit the ground and I injured my arm and I couldn't throw any more. In fact, I tried to pitch one more game before the season was over, but I couldn't throw. Being in the minor leagues, they didn't even take an X ray or send you to a doctor. I thought my arm would get better over the winter, but it sure didn't.

Rust: Let's go to 1942. I was a Cardinal fan and you guys had won forty-three of your last fifty-two ballgames to beat out the Brooklyn Dodgers. What are your memories of that 1942 campaign?

Musial: Well, I know that it was a great season, because we were behind the Dodgers something like eleven games in August. We had a good-spirited club. We had good pitching, speed, and defense, and then we got on a roll late in August. We beat the Dodgers in a home series, and then we went to Brooklyn and we beat them there in another series, and we started cutting down the lead. Every game was a pressure game. We had to win because the Dodgers were so far ahead of us. Finally, I think on the last day, why, we kept plugging and we kept winning and we won 104 games that year.

Rust: You won 106. They won 104.

Musial: That was a lot of ballgames. We were winning a lot of close ballgames, coming from behind, and we just had a great, great club. We just knew we could win. But you know, the Dodgers won 104 games. They were an outstanding club. There were great ballplayers on their club. But our club was just a little bit better.

Rust: In that period, Mort Cooper and Whitlow Wyatt were the best right-handers in major league baseball.

Musial: When we battled those Dodgers—whoever got one run seems like. . . .

Rust: They won the ballgame. . . .

Musial: They won the ballgame. We played hard baseball and we won against each other. The Dodgers had good pitching, and so did the Cardinals. So we had some great battles with the Dodgers. Playing against the Dodgers was always exciting, as you know. The fans were so energetic, and the field was close and there was a lot of excitement in the games. I enjoyed playing in Brooklyn. I really did. They were great fans.

Rust: All right. The World Series. The first game in Sportsman's Park. I can see it right now. At least I "saw" it on the radio. Red Ruffing seven and two-thirds innings of no-hit ball. Terry Moore got a bingle with two outs in the bottom of the eighth. The Yankees beat you 7-4. You scored four in the bottom of the ninth. I think you made the last out. You hit one to Buddy Hassett at first base.

Musial: Yes, I remember that one. We made such a great rally, and I came up with the bases loaded and they put in Spud Chandler. He was a sinker-ball pitcher, you know, and first I hit a hard grounder to first base. We came back and we won the next four in a row. You know, in '42 the Yankees had a really great ballclub, with Joe DiMaggio, Bill Dickey, and Red Rolfe, Phil Rizzuto, and Charlie Keller. We had a good club, and we felt that nobody could beat us. I remember that season very well because that was my rookie year and I was thrilled playing in a World Series against the New York Yankees and going to New York. That was my most thrilling year, I guess.

Rust: Stan, I saw the Saturday, Sunday, and Monday games. I saw Ernie White beat Chandler two to nothing that Saturday. A gorgeous Saturday October afternoon. I saw Terry Moore make one helluva catch. DiMaggio hit a ball to left center field, you slipped, and Terry Moore dove and caught the ball. He was at right angles to the ground. Do you remember that play?

Musial: I remember it very well. Well, I guess a lot of good fans would know, but left field in the Yankee Stadium in October is very hard. It's a very hard place to play because of the shadows and smoke. You just couldn't pick up the ball as it was hit off the bat. So I was playing in left field.

Legends

DiMaggio hit a tough drive into left center and I went for it and you couldn't hear because of the noise. I couldn't remember whether Terry Moore was hollering. . . . Anyway, I dove out of his way and slipped a little, and of course he made a one-handed catch and it was a great play for him.

Rust: I would like to know your comments on these pitchers. First, Sal Maglie.

Musial: Sal Maglie was a great competitor. He was a great pitcher for the Giants and the Dodgers. Sal had trouble beating us, the Cardinals, because we had a lot of left-hand hitters in our lineup, but Sal Maglie was a great pitcher. He was a great competitor. He would knock you down.

Rust: What about Robin Roberts?

Musial: I would say that Robin Roberts was probably the best right-hander that I ever hit against in the National League. He pitched for a lot of years and he was a great competitor and he had great control. Roberts from the right side and Warren Spahn from the left side, to me, were two of the best pitchers that I ever competed against.

Rust: Now, St. Louis has got Ozzie Smith as their shortstop. In your days was there anyone as slick with the glove as him?

Musial: I would say that guys like Peewee Reese and Phil Rizzuto and Marty Marion—they all were about equal. Of course, Ozzie is a fantastic shortstop. He gets a great jump on the ball and he has a very accurate arm. So I would say that of the fellows I saw or that I competed against, these three were—they were Smith's equal.

Rust: How about your impressions of Don Mattingly?

Musial: Well, I haven't seen him play that often. I watch him somewhat on television. Of course, you know, he has

Stan Musial

a great stroke, and he hits the ball well. Hits to all fields. Hits it where it is pitched. He can pull and hit with power. He looks to me like he is really a great outstanding hitter and he should be able to hit for many, many more years. He's a young fellow and he's very aggressive. I like his style because he goes with the pitch and doesn't give in to those pitchers. What he has done in the last two years has been phenomenal. I think two years ago he's got something like 235 hits. And last year he got well over 200, so what he did in his first two years was terrific.

Rust: Stan, I want you to elaborate on your quote when you said the secret of hitting is to relax, concentrate, and don't hit a fly ball to center field.

Musial: It's somewhat like you've got to be relaxed and not have any pressure on you. You can't be thinking about too many things. It's somewhat like what Yogi Berra said, "You can't think and hit, too!" Of course, my theory on hitting was if the ball was outside, I'd go to left field. If it was inside, I'd try to pull it and I'd try to keep away from hitting into center field because those fellows out in center field, like Bill Virdon of the Pittsburgh Pirates and Willie Mays and Duke Snider—those fellows had the best hands, they had the best feet, and they could cover a lot of ground. So I tried to keep away from the center field area, and I always hit the ball to left field or I'd try to pull it to right. That was my theory about hitting. To try to keep it away from center field.

Rust: Stanley, Kenny Heintzelman of the Pittsburgh Pirates used to give the Cardinals fits.

Musial: You know why, Art? Kenny Heintzelman had a bunch of changes and he had a slow ball. Before you knew it, he had two strikes on you. You'd want to try to hit it out of the ballpark. And, you're right, he gave the club fits. And, you're right, he beat us a lot of ballgames.

Legends

Rust: Stan, let's reminisce. Let's go back to—I "saw" this one on the radio. The first Sunday in May of 1954, a twin bill in Sportsman's Park against the New York Giants—five round-trippers for Stanley Frank Musial.

Musial: The first two were against Johnny Antonelli. He was a tough left-handed pitcher, and Johnny was a really good competitor. I hit two off him, my first two. Then I hit two off of Hoyt Wilhelm. He was a knuckleball pitcher. I didn't like to hit the knuckleballs, and I guess one of them was a knuckleball, and the other one was, I think, a kinda fastball he tried to throw past me. And the other guy I hit the home run off of was Jim Hearn. The funny part of that afternoon is that I didn't realize that I had set some kind of a record.

Rust: Let's go back to something very unpleasant. The 1947 season, the first year that Jackie Roosevelt Robinson came up with the Brooklyn Dodgers. What's the real story on your ballclub refusing to play against the Dodgers and Jackie Robinson?

Musial: When Robinson was going to play in St. Louis, they said that the rumors were that we weren't going to play, that we were going to have a strike. There was no truth to that whatsoever. They had some Southern ballplayers on our club and they were, of course—you could hear some mumbles in there—but there was no kind of boycott of any kind. That's the absolute fact and truth about the entire matter. Jackie had a great career. He was an exciting ballplayer. He led the Dodgers for many years.

Rust: Well, Ford Frick threatened your ballclub and the manager that if there was going to be no play, you were going to have a big problem.

Musial: I didn't hear anything about it. He didn't talk to us, so I am not—these are the exact facts.

Stan Musial

Rust: Did you ever have any aspirations to become a manager?

Musial: No, I didn't have any aspirations of ever becoming a manager, because you've gotta have the right physical makeup to become a manager. I don't think I would have had much patience.

Rust: Patience and material.

Musial: That helps, but no, I never had any dreams of becoming a manager. You know, a manager's job is not an easy job. You're worrying about winning and losing and trying to set aside twenty-five guys and manage them. I didn't think I'd like to have been a manager.

Rust: All right, from '41 until 1963, you played under about nine guys, starting out with one of my favorites, Billy Southworth. Let's talk about those guys.

Musial: Well, Southworth was one of them. We had a young ballclub in the 1940s, and Southworth was sort of a veteran manager at that time. He had a good rapport with the veteran ballplayers and the rookies, and he kept us on an even keel. The other guy I liked was Fred Hutchinson. He was a tough competitor. And Eddie Stanky. He was a good manager, but he just couldn't have much material in the 1950s. As a player, I didn't worry about who the manager was. I was doing the best that I could in every game, and every year I was trying to have a good year. Who the manager was didn't really matter so much, because, you know, I got along with all of them, Art. I did my job. That's the way I played.

Rust: Stanley, give me your all-time National League team. Give me two for each position, behind the plate; give me two right-handers and give me two left-handers. Let's go around the whole park. Behind the plate?

Legends

Musial: Well, of course, Campanella would be one of them right off the bat. I can think of Campy as a good defensive catcher. He could call a game and he was a good hitter. Campy, to me, was the best catcher I ever saw in the National League.

Rust: Now one more.

Musial: One more?

Rust: What about Walker Cooper?

Musial: Well, Walker wasn't that good of a defensive catcher, Art. I would say Al Lopez. But of course at first base I'll have to say—ah, John Mize and probably Ted Kluzewski; at second base, that would be Jackie Robinson and Red Schoendienst; and then at short would be Peewee Reese and Marty Marion; at third base it would be Kenny Boyer, and I can't think offhand of a next third baseman. Then I would say, in left field, I guess it would be Ralph Kiner and Roberto Clemente, and in center field, Willie Mays and Duke Snider, and in right field, it would be Henry Aaron, and now we've got to get another outfielder.

Rust: Well, that's okay. Now what about the pitcher?

Musial: The right-hander was Robin Roberts and the left-hander would be Warren Spahn. And then the other two guys I would have to put in there would be Don Drysdale and Sandy Koufax.

Rust: Not a bad quartet.

Musial: One of my great guys and, of course, I played with him, was one of the greatest, Bob Gibson.

Rust: What would you like to see in baseball, Stan, that's not there now? What about the DH?

Stan Musial

Musial: Of course, I'm against the DH. The nice thing about baseball is that everybody knows his game. There haven't been as many rule changes in baseball as there have been in other sports, you know. The pitchers are part of the game, and you know, with the DH, the manager doesn't have any strategy. I like to see a bunt. It's an exciting play in baseball. Art, in closing, I'd like to say that I'm grateful for what baseball has given me, in recognition, records, thrills, money, and tons of memories.

5

Warren Spahn

THE *first time I saw Warren Spahn he pitched at the old Polo Grounds in 1942, when the Boston Braves played the New York Giants. Casey Stengel brought him out of the bullpen in the eighth inning with the Braves trailing. Babe Barna greeted him with a three-run triple, but Boston won the game. They won it on a forfeit.*

There were thousands of us kids in the Polo Grounds that day. Yes, I was one of them. We got in by bringing a few items of scrap iron or aluminum for the war effort. When he got the side out in the eighth, kids—yours truly included—swarmed onto the field and wouldn't clear it even under the threat of forfeit to the visiting club. So the umpires finally awarded the game to the Braves.

Even on first view, I could see that this hawk-nosed, high-kicking, smooth-throwing, and stylish southpaw had what it took to be a great one.

Spahn had one distinction I'll never forget. In my mind's eye, I recall him as the only pitcher to walk a batter to get to Stan Musial. It was back in '57, when the St. Louis Cardinals were playing Milwaukee for the league lead. Spahn came in from the bullpen in the ninth inning to protect Milwaukee's one-run lead. He walked the batter in

Warren Spahn

front of Musial to set up an inning-ending double play. And Musial obliged.

Warren is a comedian. A wise-cracking kind of guy.

Rust: Warren, the first time I saw you was at the Polo Grounds in 1942. What are your memories of that day?

Spahn: I remember it very well because it was one of the first times that I pitched in the big leagues. I couldn't imagine what was happening. It was in the eighth—the seventh inning. They had let young people in the ballpark with x-numbers of . . .

Rust: Scrap iron, aluminum, whatever.

Spahn: And they were up in the upper deck. In the seventh inning they came down to the first tier and then, of course, they came out onto the field. There were thousands of them on the field. And the announcer told them that if they didn't get off in a certain period of time that the game was going to be forfeited. Oh, I did get the side out, yes, and Boston won the ballgame, nine to nothing. And I was hoping that I would get the victory, but that doesn't work that way. All those records are in the record book, except for the winning pitcher and the losing pitcher.

Rust: It says zero and zero for Spahnie then in 1942?

Spahn: Right.

Rust: All right, Spahnie, the first time—the first time I recall seeing your name I was reading the *Sporting News* in '40, and I saw the name Spahn, with Bradford, in the Class D Pony League. What are your memories of your first year as a professional ballplayer?

Legends

Spahn: Well, I came in there after I graduated from high school, and it was my first experience away from home, though only about ninety miles away. I remember getting off the train and it suddenly hit me that I was away from home and that I was a professional. And I think I pitched in about, oh, I don't know, twelve or thirteen games. I hurt my elbow trying to throw an unorthodox curveball, and it probably was the luckiest break I ever got, because the Braves invited me to spring training the following year to see if my arm was all right. I got an opportunity to pitch in the spring training and to be indoctrinated with all the greats that I remember about in the big leagues. Like Ernie Lombardi and Manny Salvo and Si Johnson and all those guys. I was hoping against hope that I might stay with the big league club, but they dropped me off at Evansville when we played an exhibition game, which was their Class B ballclub.

Rust: You hit well enough to stay in a ballgame, because you could swing the stick. You were a helluva fielder, a superb fielder. You ran the bases well and your move to first base was brilliant. Now I remember a game up in Boston, I think it was around Labor Day of '48—you picked off Jackie Robinson twice in a vital game. You know, Jackie, at that time, was the greatest base stealer in major league baseball. What are your memories of that?

Spahn: It seemed that Jackie had a problem with my move, and, yes, he was a great base stealer. I think the significant thing about it is that I picked Jackie off twice in that ballgame, and he never tried to steal on me again, which is a heck of an asset. You know, any time a guy steals second base, he's a potential run. Any time you've got a man on first base, he's a potential double play. The Dodgers had always had great people, and when you thwart one of them, such as Jackie Robinson . . . I was pleased and delighted that

68

the Dodgers really didn't try stealing on me. That's the benefit of the reputation of having a good move.

Rust: Let's evaluate first, Billy Southworth.

Spahn: Well, Billy was a very sound, fundamental baseball manager, and I feel very close to him because he gave me an opportunity to pitch. He started me and he remembered me when he was with the Cardinals to give me an opportunity to pitch in Boston. You know, there is no perfect manager, and I sort of feel like I managed for five years. A good manager is a lousy one without horses, so players make managers. Managers don't win the games, players do.

Rust: Okay, what about Charley Grimm?

Spahn: Hey, if you couldn't play for Charley Grimm, you couldn't play for anybody. Charley was a lovable guy, he definitely was a baseball player's manager. Opening day of the season, he'd say, "This is the bat, the ball, and the glove; now, go get 'em!" You know, we didn't have intricate signs, we didn't pull inside things—just go out and get 'em.

Rust: In 1948 with the Boston Braves it was you and Johnny Sain, and then Bill Voiselle and Vern Bickford. What are your memories of that '48 campaign?

Spahn: Well, I remember that we had an older ballclub. We beat some pretty good ballclubs in the National League, and I remember talking to John Carmichael from Chicago, who was a very astute baseball person. I said, "Hey, John, what are our chances against Cleveland in the World Series?" And he said, "Your chances are like a snowball in hell. Your ballclub is old, and it is held together with a drop of glue and a pin." I was kind of proud of that ballclub, though. We played them close, we lost four games to two, but every ballgame was nip and tuck.

Legends

Rust: I saw Whitey Ford beat you at the Stadium in 1957. What are your memories of that World Series?

Spahn: Well, two very close ballclubs. In '57, we beat the Yankees four games to three.

Rust: Burdette had the hat trick, huh?

Spahn: In '58 they beat us four games to three. We had them beat three games to one, but couldn't pull it out. I think every time I pitched in a World Series, I was pitching against Whitey Ford, and that son of a gun was tough.

Rust: What about Lew Burdette winning those three ballgames in '57?

Spahn: Lew was a great pitcher. I think he pitched two shutouts, and maybe gave up one run in the other one, so that he had a fantastic earned-run average during that World Series. The ironic thing about it is that he would never have won three ballgames had I not come up with the flu. I was supposed to pitch in the seventh game, and I guess it was better that Lew pitched it because he pitched a shutout. Lew was rather fidgety, and also I think that Lew was a great athlete. He was tough and he was burly, and he could do a lot of things. He swung the bat well. I think his determination was such an asset, and, he kept the ball low, he was tough, he didn't give up too many home runs—just a heck of a competitor.

Rust: What's your feeling, your enjoyments, of touring the country now with other Old Timers and being able to bring the fans some of the enjoyment in seeing some of their old-time favorites?

Spahn: Well, I am very proud of my association with the Equitable group. We have an old-timer's series that has a great purpose, and the Equitable is donating $10,000 for each ballgame in twenty-six cities. So we are netting $260,000 that we use to take care of the people that are either down on their luck or financially insecure. We have an organization in the commissioner's office called "BAT," and that stands for Baseball Alumni Teams. Our sole purpose is to see that those funds are distributed among the needy, and also we hope to do something toward a retreat for old-time ballplayers. Maybe some day in the sunshine we can get old pitchers and old hitters together and they can lie to each other about curveballs and line drives. We are going to continue it in the coming years. We have a great deal of camaraderie. We have an amazing number of people that participate in these ballgames, I think there are over 600 of them. It's a great way to rub elbows, to renew old friendships, it's like weekend outings, more or less. I think the people in the United States have appreciated what we are trying to do because we have drawn a lot of people into the ballparks.

Rust: How do you feel about how the writers and how they select some players and ignore some others for the Hall of Fame?

Spahn: Well, we have a number of baseball writers and to be eligible to vote for the Hall of Fame you have to have been a baseball writer for like ten years. A lot of the writers of today haven't seen some of these old guys play, and who says who should be there and who shouldn't be. It's a tough situation. I, for one, feel like my roommate, Lew Burdette, should have been in there a long time ago. I feel that anybody that does something like Roger Maris hitting 61 home runs or Hank Aaron hitting enough home runs to lead in the history of home runs hit, they should go in automatically. Why should they have to wait five years?

But we have rules, and I think those rules should be abided by. I, for one, am very proud of the fact that I was elected the first time I was eligible, but a lot of guys are out there that have credentials to be in there. I hope it's not a personality contest. I think that credentials are the thing that should put a guy into the Hall of Fame. I remember guys like—I'll give you a good example, Bobby Doerr.

Rust: It took him a long time, didn't it?

Spahn: Bobby Doerr had great credentials, and he just got voted in last year (1986)—voted in by the Old Timers' Committee in their election. And I'll never know why in the world he wasn't elected prior to this.

Rust: Well, that's why they have the old-timers', the veterans' committee, to vote these guys in, the fellows that these young writers really never saw play.

Spahn: I am very proud of the era that I played in. Many of the media people have called it the Golden Age. I still think the guys that are playing today are just making us more popular. So many people are playing now in the big leagues that are probably only really Triple A ballclub players because of expansion. I am concerned about the history of baseball and keeping it on a high plateau.

Rust: Who was the toughest batter for you, Warren? What about your battles with Stan Musial—what were they like?

Spahn: He hit .300 off of me, like he did off anybody else. I made heroes out of guys you never even heard of. But the bottom line. . . .

Rust: Well, I would have heard of them—just give me the names. Who gave you the hardest times?

Spahn: All right, Curt Roberts. Do you remember Curt Roberts?

Rust: I certainly do.

Warren Spahn

Spahn: The Pittsburgh second baseman . . .

Rust: The first black ballplayer with the Pittsburgh Pirates . . .

Spahn: Probably he hit about .189 in his career, but he would hit me well. And also, Joe Cunningham, who played with the St. Louis Cardinals.

Rust: St. Louis, their first baseman.

Spahn: He probably hit me better than Musial did. Gordy Coleman who played with Cincinnati—another left-hander. It just seems like certain hitters have the timing that's similar to the pitcher's timing, and I think they see the ball better.

Rust: Do you remember Mike Goliat—he could hit the hell out of Don Newcombe?

Spahn: Goliat? I am amazed that Goliat hit .300. He was around a couple of years, and then he disappeared. And he wasn't that bad a ballplayer.

Rust: Who were the best eight players that you played against that you saw in the '40s?

Spahn: Holy cow! People like Jackie Robinson, Gil Hodges, Roberto Clemente, Stan Musial, you know, all the formidable players that have been heralded, I think were great ballplayers. It's like comparing apples and oranges. Wouldn't you like to have all of those people on your same ballclub? Every ballclub had like two or three of these guys who were great ballplayers. I can think of Kenny Boyer with St. Louis, along with Musial; Cincinnati had their great people, and of course the Giants did too—Philadelphia, you know, right down the line—there were great ballplayers on every ballclub.

Legends

Rust: What changes have you seen in the development of pitchers—or in pitching in major league baseball?

Spahn: I think the curveball has been neglected. I think that we played hard-nose baseball, and everybody is a gentleman now because you make your million and I'll make mine and nobody gets hurt. I think the umpires have enforced that a pitcher doesn't pitch inside. I'm not talking about knocking guys down but pitching on the inside part of the plate. I totally feel that there isn't a hitter that gets hit by a pitcher—it's the fact that they don't get out of the way of it. Now they don't know how to get out of the way. I think it's a fallacy that we protect the guys that literally intimidate pitchers, and I think that Reggie Jackson is a good example.

Rust: What do you think the reason is that Rizzuto is not in the Hall of Fame and Pee Wee Reese is?

Spahn: Probably Phil Rizzuto has cried so much about it that he has turned a lot of people off. Pee Wee was the captain of the Dodgers, and I think that Brooks Robinson being inducted probably opened the door for the defensive ballplayers. Phil Rizzuto played on some great ballclubs that could afford to carry him. And I'm not voting against Phil Rizzuto. But everything seems to go in waves, and Phil has cried so much about being overlooked that maybe he has turned some people off.

Rust: How much doctoring of the ball was done and is being done in major league competition?

Spahn: I know guys that threw the spitter. Now we're getting more sophisticated. I think there are a lot of people playing around with the baseball. And I don't feel that any umpire in the big leagues is going to point his finger at a pitcher and say you're throwing an illegal pitch. We tried

74

everything, declaring it a no-pitch, and everything. But originally, after Cleveland Indian shortstop Ray Chapman was killed by a spitball by New York Yankees submarine artist Carl Mays at the Polo Grounds in 1920, any time that you doctored the baseball, it was suspension from baseball permanently. I don't think that any of the umpires want to tell a guy—you know, deprive him of a way of making a living, but I think it could be policed a lot better than it is. There are legitimate pitches. A split-fingered fastball, to me, is nothing more than a fork ball. I think a lot of people are playing with the thing, you know, to use foreign substances, to cut the ball, and that should be detected.

Rust: Dwight Gooden. What's your evaluation of him?

Spahn: Well, Dwight Gooden is a great athlete. He has poise, he has got control, he has got good stuff.

Rust: Does success contribute to problems off the field?

Spahn: Pride of accomplishment, I think, is a big thing, but I also think that we are only mortals, human beings, and that a man should be very, very happy about God-given talent. He should be able to do it as long as youth will allow it. Anybody who gets affected by it is crazy.

Rust: Joe Adcock and Eddie Matthews. Your comments on them.

Spahn: Eddie Matthews was a great home run hitter. Also, the kind of guy that asked no quarter and gave none when he played. I think we had a ballclub that had pranksters and whatever, but when they got between the two white lines, it was all business. Joe Adcock was a big, strong guy that looked for pitches and when he guessed right, he was dynamite. And he was great on thrown balls. He wasn't that great as a fielder on ground balls, but the collection of ballplayers that we had in Milwaukee, I'd say in a five-year period—it was a great ballclub. In addition to Adcock, Matthews, Aaron, we had Johnny Logan, Red Schoendienst, Billy Bruton, Del Crandall, to name a few.

Rust: You won 363 ballgames in your career. It might have been over 400 if you didn't go into the military.

Spahn: I lost three-and-a-half years in the Army. I can reflect to our young society, and I remember when I was a kid that our nation was in trouble and that if you didn't serve your country you were square. In today's society if you do things like that, you're square, and it's the hip thing to do to get out of responsibility, or whatever. I didn't want to be a serviceman, but my country was in trouble and I spent three-and-a-half years, but I think that I grew up. I think that it made me a better pitcher.

I think I was able to perform under stress better than I did before I went into the service, and I think it was the training that I had gotten in the service. There are a helluva bunch of guys out there who are on welfare that would do themselves and their country a favor by going into the military. It's a great learning experience. In addition, you can be proud of being an American, and I never once felt that I was deprived. I felt that I came back with a different allegiance to the game, and to my country, and I did play until I was 44. Maybe I was physically better able to endure that long because I was in the service.

Rust: I think you once told us a story about how you tried to throw the spitball—and what happened.

Spahn: I threw one spitball in my career. Lew Burdette showed me how to do it. I worked for two or three months on it and I threw one to a guy by the name of Walt Moiyn of the Cubs in Chicago.

Rust: And where did it wind up?

Spahn: It wound up in the right center field bleachers for a home run. As Walt came around third base, I said, "Walt, do you know that you hit a spitter?" and he said, "Yeah, but it didn't spit!" And I tucked that thing in my back pocket and I never used it again.

Rust: Your comments about Richie Ashburn. He's not in the Hall of Fame in Cooperstown.

Spahn: I think Richie played center field with a lot of other people who played it not as well defensively perhaps, but I think he had better stats as far as home runs, base hits, and batting average. Richie, you know, played an extremely great center field. He had a big one to cover, and he was a base-on-balls guy. He was on base all the time. He could run and steal bases but was not really a home run threat. I don't know, I'm not going to get into selection of people for the Hall of Fame, but I think when you are talking in the area of center field, you are thinking about guys like Joe DiMaggio, Mickey Mantle, and all the great people who have played center field, and . . .

Rust: I notice that you didn't say Terry Moore.

Spahn: Well, Terry was another great guy, but probably he didn't have the stats of the other people that played center field.

Rust: He was a .280 hitter.

Spahn: I know, but .280 doesn't get it. I think you had people who played better, who hit .320, .340, or better. If you're going to talk Terry Moore, Richie Ashburn, how about the guy that played center field for Pittsburgh?

Rust: Billy Virdon.

Spahn: Billy Virdon—probably one of the classic center fielders.

Legends

Rust: He was.

Spahn: Billy Bruton, who played on my ballclub. He could go get 'em. You can go on and on and on about great center fielders who had good arms and could go get the ball. When you talk about putting all the stats together, there have been some great people that have played center field.

Rust: But, listen, don't you feel, Warren, that there is a great inequity if a guy is not a good all-around ballplayer to be in the Hall of Fame? You've got a lot of hitters in that Hall of Fame—and I'm not going to name the names—who couldn't catch a baseball if you put it in their glove.

Spahn: I agree with you.

Rust: So, isn't defense very, very important?

Spahn: Of course it is. And I am not an advocate of the DH, and there are going to be some DH's that get into the Hall of Fame. If we are going to put DH's into the Hall of Fame, then I think that we ought to have offense and defense in baseball as well as football. And why the hell do we pick on pitchers? There's a lot of good pitchers that don't get a chance to get up to the plate because somebody said we gotta support DH's. I'm thinking of guys like Tom Seaver, for one.

Rust: He can hit, yeah.

Spahn: And Lefty Steve Carlton, and guys who are good athletes. Bob Gibson was a helluva athlete, and I am thankful that there wasn't a DH around for him. And I feel that I would be perturbed if somebody else went up there to hit for me. I wasn't a good hitter, but I loved to run the bases. Any kid that plays in the Little League knows that the fun in the game is in swinging the bat and in hitting the ball. And when you hit the ball well, it's a feeling that you will never forget, and yet we came up with this insidious thing of a DH for the pitcher. Why the hell don't we ever put in a DH for the shortstop? There are guys there hitting .112 who are playing shortstop. We ought to have two DH's, and then let's go to three, and let's go to offensive teams and defensive teams in baseball. I think it would take something away from it.

Rust: Did Ashburn give you a hard time?

Spahn: Yes, he did. I can remember one ballgame where he fouled off like 24 pitches, and, God, he must have killed a lot of fans. I know he cost the Philadelphia Phillies a lot of money in baseballs. And, yeah, he made you work hard. Hell, you'd face Ashburn the first time in the ballgame and you'd throw 30 pitches to him, and you'd think about the ninth inning, and you'd think, hey, I'm going to be a lot more tired in the ninth inning against this little son of a gun than I would be if I were pitching against another club.

Rust: Hey, Warren, I'm at the Polo Grounds one night in May of 1951 when Willie Mays went 0 for April and May —0 for April and May literally—and he hit the ball over the left-field roof. What are your memories of that night?

Spahn: Do I remember it? I was the first person in the National League or baseball lore that realized that Willie Mays was a good hitter.

Rust: Well, what kind of pitch was it?

Spahn: It was a curveball. It was on the outside part of the plate, and, you know, weaknesses go around the league like wildfire. The story was that Willie couldn't handle the ball if it was down and away from him, but they forgot to tell me that it was from a right-hander, not a left-hander.

Rust: He hit it over the roof, baby.

Legends

Spahn: No, it wasn't over the roof, it knocked three seats out. I knew before anybody that Willie Mays was a good hitter, and I think he proved it when he was inducted into the Hall of Fame. I told him that he would have never made it without me.

6

Eddie
Stanky

EDDIE was a gutsy little
SOB. That's really the best description I can give him.
Didn't have much talent but what he had was knowledge.
He was a baseball brain. He just knew how to beat the
hell out of you.

I'll never forget Stanky dropkicking the ball from the
glove of Phil Rizzuto in the World Series.

They called him "The Brat" and it fit him perfectly.
He was a scrappy little guy with a nasty attitude. He re-
minded me of one of those little pit bulls. When he was
riled, then he was most dangerous.

Rust: Eddie, you played for three different pennant winners, the '47 Dodgers, the '48 Boston Braves, and the '51
New York Giants. I was there the day of the Bobby Thomson
game in October of 1951. The first picture I have in my
memory, in my mind's eye, when Bobby hit the ball into
the seats, is of you jumping on top of Leo Durocher.

Stanky: That was one of the biggest thrills in all my years
of baseball. We came back from 13½ games behind in Au-

gust and we tied the great Dodger ballclub. Then we beat them two out of three with Bobby Thomson's home run.

We were three runs behind going into the ninth inning, and then we got a couple of base hits. Then Bobby came up and hit that home run. I was out of my mind for the next forty minutes, they tell me. Now, a lot of people don't believe this, but Leo Durocher and I have a wonderful association. I was very happy—not just for myself or the team, but for Leo, the manager. The only other thing that I could remember was going and jumping on Leo, saying "We did it! We did it! We did it!" Art, I had the pleasure of playing with some great ballclubs, but this New York Giant team of 1951—we had the best glue, or togetherness as they call it, of any ballclub I had ever been on.

Rust: Let's talk about the mound staff or Larry Jansen and Sal Maglie.

Stanky: Oh, they were tough pitchers. I mean, they were great pitchers to a point. When the big game had to be won, they wanted to be on the mound. Now, they were of two different personalities. Larry Jansen was an easy-going, laughable person when he was pitching. If he was behind, he would be laughing and saying, "All right, boys, let's get a run." Sal Maglie you could not talk to during a ballgame. I would go out, maybe in a tough situation . . . I would leave my position at second base and go to talk to Sal when he was pitching, and I would say, "Sal, let's calm down now, let's calm down." He would say, "You get back to your position: I'll get him out." You could not talk to the Old Barber during a ballgame.

Rust: What about Jim Hearn?

Stanky: Jim Hearn was one of the young fellows on the squad but he had a great curveball. A very emotional boy, very emotional, but when he was not pitching he would be in the ballgame rooting for everybody. Maglie was different. He would sit back in the corner and wouldn't say anything to anybody, even when he was not pitching. But, that was a great pitching staff. Like I keep repeating, it was a great ballclub, a great bunch of guys, the best ballclub for togetherness. We had five active fellows who went on to manage in the major leagues on that ballclub. Think of it. The guys on that 1951 ballclub who became managers, besides me, were Whitey Lockman, Al Dark, Wes Westrum, and Bill Rigney.

Rust: What about Willie Mays? That same year, 1951, was Willie's first year in the majors.

Stanky: Oh, Willie Mays—and Willie Mays, I thought, would be the first black manager, Art. He had leadership. He knew how to handle people. He was intelligent and a great, great ballplayer. It is true, when he first came up from Minneapolis, he went 12 times to bat without a base hit.

Rust: Until he hit that ball off of Warren Spahn.

Stanky: Warren Spahn. Yes, out of the ballpark.

Rust: Over the roof, yes.

Stanky: . . . hey, you've got a good memory, too, Art.

Rust: I was there that night.

Stanky: Hey, fella, you didn't miss many games out there. But Willie Mays was the first player out on the ballfield and the last one to leave it . . . even when he became a superstar. He never lost his zest for the game or his ability to communicate with rookies. He was the first one playing pepper. He had a lot of fun out on the field. When I left the ballclub to manage the St. Louis Cardinals—this was after the 1951 season—I received a fine package from Willie Mays. It was a beautiful, beautiful, alpaca sweater with a note, which I still have in my office . . . he used to call me "Skip." It said: "Thanks, Skip, for what you have done when I first came up." It was a beautiful note and it came from a class guy!

Rust: All right, what about the '48 Boston ballclub? You and Earl Torgeson and, let me see—ah, Bob Elliott, Tommy Holmes, Mike McCormick, and . . .

Stanky: Phil Masi.

Rust: Yeah, and Jeff Heath . . . Warren Spahn, Johnny Sain, Vern Bickford, and Bill Voiselle.

Stanky: I was traded in March of 1948 from the Dodgers to the Boston Braves in a trade a lot of people did not like —including myself at the time. But I was traded to a great ballclub. Billy Southworth was the manager, and I was having a super year. At that time Durocher and I were not talking to each other. This was due to my being traded. He said something to the press that I was not worth the salary that I was asking and I took offense to this. In an immature way I did not talk to Durocher.

So all during the Series, a lot of photographers asked for me to pose with Leo, after I was traded to Boston, but I would say no. As luck would have it, I got off to a good start, but I broke my ankle. I played in only 67 games. We played Cleveland in the World Series that year. They had a great pitcher named Gene Beardon, and of course Bob Feller was also there, and Bob Lemon. They defeated the Braves four out of six games.

Rust: Let's talk about your first series, in '47.

Stanky: What a thrill. Leo Durocher had been suspended for associating with "undesirable people," as they put it. Burt Shotton kindly took over.

Rust: Burt "Civilian Clothes" Shotton.

Eddie Stanky

Stanky: That's right, a fine gentleman, but he was just 100 percent the opposite of Leo. Well, anyway we win the pennant. Then the ballplayers vote to see how we chop up the money. I brought up Leo Durocher's name. I thought Leo had worked with us through spring training, that this was his ballclub.

Rust: He put the ballclub together.

Stanky: But the commissioner, Happy Chandler, voted our full share for Leo out of the picture. He would not allow it. But we thought so much of Leo. We voted Leo a full share of our 1947 World Series money.

Rust: The first year of Jackie Roosevelt Robinson. How did you get along with Jackie?

Stanky: All right . . . in 1947.

Rust: And tell me the truth, now, Eddie.

Stanky: I'll tell you the truth, Art. I never played against Ty Cobb, of course, but Jackie Robinson was one of the best baserunners I ever saw in using his own judgment. He was really always a threat, Art. In 1947 Jackie Robinson led the league in getting hit by pitches.

Rust: Yes, he crowded the plate.

Stanky: Not only that, but they were taking shots at him. Jackie got off to a very poor start, but luckily we were winning. We were winning and naturally you don't change a winning line-up. Jackie Robinson played first base and I played second base. There was a couple of ballplayers that did not like Jackie being on the ballclub.

Rust: Yes, now that is an understatement, because . . .

Stanky: We had accepted Jackie because he was a very good fellow . . . one of the real men, and above all, he had good talent. He was a major leaguer. We knew that. We could see that . . . so, he helped us to win the pennant. The last three months of the season, he was a championship ballplayer. It was a pleasure playing alongside of Jackie. And then, due to the fact that he was a second baseman, that was one of the main reasons I was traded from the Dodgers to the Boston Braves at the end of the '47 season.

Rust: Eddie, your breaking up of Ewell Blackwell's no-hitter in 1947. I will never forget that one.

Stanky: Ewell Blackwell was trying to do what Vander Meer did, pitch two consecutive no-hitters. This was in Cincinnati, the first game of a doubleheader. Blackwell gets one out in the ninth inning, and I come up. I hit a ball—you had to see it to believe it—which should have been fielded by Blackwell.

Rust: It went right under his glove.

Stanky: But, as you know, he fell towards third base and the ball trickled through the mound, over second base. I don't think it got three feet out in the grass—it was just a cheap hit. But it broke up the poor fellow's no-hitter. Now, we lose the ballgame, of course. To get to our clubhouse, we had to go through the stands in the old Crosley Field. And those women were hitting me with their pocketbooks as I was going into the clubhouse. I'll never forget it. Calling me everything in the book, hitting me with pocketbooks over the head, but I did get a real cheap hit, and Blackwell was a tough pitcher.

Rust: He was a mean hombre coming by way of third base.

Stanky: That is correct.

Rust: Several years ago, in 1977 to be exact, you come back as the manager of the Texas Rangers, and you quit after one game. What happened, Eddie?

Stanky: I'm glad that you brought that up, Art. I'm coaching at the University of South Alabama, and the Texas team was thinking of making a change of managers. Am I interested? This was on a Friday night. This is the owner of the ballclub calling me, and I said, "Well, I won't tell you no . . . let me talk it over with my wonderful wife." So I hang up and my wife and I spent until two o'clock the next morning discussing the possibilities . . . and as always I have a very understanding wife regarding baseball.

She said, "Well, honey, whatever you want to do, do what you want." So we figured out what would be the best contract, and so forth, and, to make a long story short, all the dignitaries, the vice presidents, and everybody flew in from Mobile, unbeknownst to any of the press or anything. I had rented a private room in a restaurant where we could sit and have a dinner and discuss everything. So they came down on a Monday and we sat there for three or four hours, and I came up with a fine contract. It would take care of me for five years, with a guarantee that I would stay on as a consultant as long as I wanted at $50,000 a year after I was through managing. Now, it was an ideal thing, set up for my whole family.

I agree to terms and I come back. My wife had a glass of champagne, and all the children and I were celebrating. I fly out that Wednesday under an assumed name to join the ballclub in Minneapolis. I traveled under the name of Dr. Greene. How I came up with that I don't know.

Rust: What was your first name?

Stanky: I didn't have one. They meet me at the Minneapolis Airport and now it's about 5:30 at night and we've got a night game scheduled. Gene Mauch is the manager of the Minneapolis Twins. They asked me to meet with my ballplayers. I had a little short meeting with the ballplayers. Connie Ryan is my coach, whom I know since we were teammates on the old Boston Braves. We were in for a tough ballgame. We have the bases loaded in the ninth inning, with the tying run at the plate, and I bring in Mike Marshall, a great relief pitcher. I can't remember who the fellow was, but he was leading his club in home runs at Minneapolis, and Mike Marshall ran the count to 3-and-2 and struck the fellow out. We win the ballgame and I am happy.

I am riding back on the bus to the hotel and I call my wife, tell her about the game, and then it hit me. I was lonesome. I was homesick. I had brought my dad home and my mother had passed away in 1972.

I guess, Art, I was very foolish. So I was thinking it was over and I decided that this was enough for me. So I waited until around six-thirty in the morning to call my wife. I didn't want to call her at two or three o'clock in the morning when I actually made up my mind. I didn't want to disturb her. So I called my wife and I said, "I'm coming home." She said, "What's the matter, what happened?" I said, "Nothing's the matter." She said, "Well, do what you want, but make sure you call the proper authorities and explain things to them."

I went to the airport, because I knew that if I had stayed at the hotel, they would have tried to influence me to remain with the club. I called the people from the airport. To make a long story short, I should never have accepted terms; I should never have left the University of South Alabama. I knew that I had too many things at home . . . my family, my children, my grandchildren. And, after that I had heart surgery; I had two valves replaced. I knew that if I had continued managing the Texas Rangers I would have ended up in the grave.

Rust: You put your values in the proper place, didn't you, Eddie?

Stanky: That is correct, and I am just glad that the good Lord gave me enough courage when I made that decision to act immediately.

Rust: How did you get that name? I mean, "The Brat"?

Stanky: There was a newspaper man named Eddie Murphy when I first came to play for the Dodgers in 1944. He worked for the old *New York Sun*. One of the nicest newspaper men in the world. And one of the first few games when we beat Boston 3-2, and I happened to get a couple of walks, and I scored all three of our runs . . .

I was born in Philadelphia, Pennsylvania, in a tough neighborhood called Kensington. You had either to be able to run fast or fight . . . so, doing his little story, he said the "Brat" from Kensington scored three runs, and so forth. And lo and behold, with an easy-going blue-eyed, non-tempered fellow like myself, they called me "The Brat" after that. That was the only reason, but off the field I prided myself on being a rather pretty good guy.

Rust: Now, how can you resolve that with Phil Rizzuto?

Stanky: It was not that I made a good play. It was the fact that Phil Rizzuto, the great shortstop for the New York Yankees, Casey Stengel's little Bobo, made a very, very poor play. They had me thrown out by 10 or 15 feet.

It was in the third game of the 1951 World Series at the Polo Grounds. Jim Hearn beat Vic Raschi 6-2. The Giants broke the game open by scoring five runs in the bottom of the fifth. In the bottom of the fifth I walked. Then I attempted to steal second. Yogi Berra made a perfect throw.

Yogi Berra, the smart catcher for the Yankees . . . we had the hit-and-run on with Al Dark . . . the fellow pitched out, and, as you know, as Branch Rickey said, I could not run too well. They had me thrown out by 10 or 15 feet, and Rizzuto had time to take the ball out of his glove and tag me bare-handed, but he gave me what I call the American League tag. He just laid the glove down, and due to the fact that I played soccer in Philadelphia, I kicked the ball, and centerfielder Joe DiMaggio fielded it. May I repeat this . . . it was not a dirty play. Anyway, I went to third. Then the floodgates opened. After a couple of walks, Whitey Lockman hit a home run.

Rust: Evaluate Branch Rickey as an executive and Leo Durocher as a manager.

Stanky: Art, I'll take the good and the bad. I'll take the bad first . . . Mr. Rickey. Mr. Rickey no doubt had a great baseball mind, but he loved money, and he did not like anybody else to have it. I wasn't making much money then, but we had one baby and I was expecting another one, and I pleaded with Mr. Rickey for a $5000 raise. No sir, no sir, I have Dixie Walker, who led the leagues in RBIs, and so forth. He gave me five thousand reasons. So he put the contract in front of me, and I said, "Mr. Rickey, I can't sign that." He said, "Get out, I don't want to look at you again." I am going out and Branch Rickey, Jr., who was a fine man . . .

Rust: They called him "The Twig" . . .

Stanky: I am going out and he said I made his dad mad. I said, "I'm trying to get some money for my family." Now I go back to Mobile, Alabama, and I don't hear anything for three weeks.

So, finally, Rickey calls me up and he says, "All right, I'm going to give you your money, but you go on down to spring training and join the ballclub," which I did. They traded me while I was in spring training to the Boston Braves. That was in 1948. Rickey said at a Rotary banquet before the season opened . . . he said I couldn't field, I couldn't throw, but I was one of the best players, and so forth. Now he was great with words but not great with money. I could not get any raise.

Rust: All right now, how about Leo Durocher?

Stanky: When I retired in South Alabama as a coach down here three years ago, Leo Durocher came from California to be with me for my last ballgame at South Alabama. He spent three days here and we reminisced. He brought up some things that I had forgotten about . . . that I had done for him as a player.

Listen to this, Art, I don't think there was ever a manager and a ballplayer—Durocher as manager and me as a ballplayer—that ever had the respect and love for each other as he and I. We knew each other. We had misunderstandings about the game, but I learned a great deal from Leo as manager. It was easy to play for Leo Durocher. All he would ask of you is to be alert, hustle, play to win, and you had no problem. Now the fellows that could not get along with Leo were those who were the crybabies. Yeah, Leo could chew you out . . . he did not care where it was, whether it be riding on the train or in a restaurant or on the ballfield or in the locker room. He didn't pick his spots, but the best manager I ever played for in the major leagues was Leo Durocher.

7

Rachael Robinson

*W*HEN *I met Rachael Robinson in 1947, I realized then and there that she was the glue that held Jackie Robinson together. There is no doubt in my mind that Jackie could not have withstood the pressure and the stress without her presence.*

Rust: Rachael, tell us first about the Jack Robinson Foundation. What's it all about?

Mrs. R: In 1973 I incorporated a foundation, mainly to perpetuate Jackie's name and his memory and his spirit. We also wanted to continue the work that he had begun, so the purpose of the foundation is to provide educational opportunities for young people who are going to college. We support them through four years of college. We provide them with funds, and we provide them with counseling. We have a hot line to our office. We are doing summer internships and job development for our graduates, and we have a networking weekend in New York where we bring all of the students who have graduated. By following them, we get to know them very well. We help them take on some of the tasks and the responsibilities that we think students can have. Because they should give back. We treat them royally, and we expect them to give back. And they do give back in big ways. We hope we are developing leaders while we are helping to educate them.

Rust: Where did you first meet Jackie Roosevelt?

Mrs. R: I met Jackie at UCLA. I was a freshman and he was a senior, and we were introduced by a mutual friend, Ray Bartlett. We were engaged by the second year. He left UCLA and went on to other things. We were engaged for five years before we married.

Rust: All right. Jackie, I know, was at Fort Riley in Kansas with Joseph Louis Barrow. And then—it's never been clear to me why he was out of the army in 1944. What happened there?

Mrs. R: Well, he was discharged after his court-martial. I think that was the basic thing, that he was considered a trouble-maker.

Rust: Recalcitrant.

Mrs. R: Not suitable material, or whatever you want to call it.

Rust: You know, he just didn't take any nonsense, that's what it was.

Mrs. R: They did have—ostensibly, they had a reason. His unit was going overseas and he had bone chips in his ankles, and so they used that as a reason. Actually, he was let go.

Rust: All right. Then he joins the Kansas City Monarchs. Do you want to take it from there?

Mrs. R: Well, he joined the Kansas City Monarchs. He was scouted by Clyde Sukeforth, and ultimately he was interviewed by Mr. Rickey and given the opportunity to play for Montreal.

Rust: All right, let me say what I can remember in my mind's eye. Let's go back. I think it was the middle of April in 1945. Jack goes up to Fenway Park along with Sam Jethroe—Sam was playing with the Cleveland Buckeyes at the time—and Marvin Williams, who was with the Philadelphia Stars. They had a tryout in front of Joseph Cronin, the old Red Sox shortstop and pilot/mentor. What were Jack's experiences there? What did he tell you about that?

Mrs. R: I don't think he put much stock in that as a real tryout. If you remember, the black press was doing a good job of crusading for a black to enter baseball. And so, Jack was carrying out the wishes of the black press and giving it a try, but he didn't feel he had a real tryout. He didn't think he had much of a chance. There was no receptivity on their part. It was just another minor disappointment, not a major one.

Rust: Rachael, just at about the same time, when the Dodgers had their training camp I believe up at Bear Mountain, I believe Joe Bostic—my good friend Joe Bostic—brought Sammy Jethroe and ... oh, no, it was Terris McDuffie from the Newark Eagles, a pitcher, and the New York Cubans first sacker, Dave "Showboat" Thomas, for a tryout. And Rickey said, no, they're not good enough. You know about that, don't you?

Mrs. R: I have heard the story. I never got it first-hand.

Rust: All right. When did Rickey first contact Jackie?

Mrs. R: That's when he was playing with the Kansas City Monarchs. Actually Clyde Sukeforth did invite him to come to New York to meet with Rickey. That was his first en-counter with Mr. Rickey.

Rust: That was August of '45—the famous meeting, the meeting at Rickey's office in dear old Brooklyn. When Jackie came home, what did he tell you about that experience?

Mrs. R: Well, he was very excited. He was excited more by the opportunity than by some of the things that have been reported. You know, the legend is that—it was not just a legend, it actually happened, but it gets repeated over and over again—that Mr. Rickey took Jack through certain role playing. What would you do if . . . ? It was to alert him to the conditions. When you are going into a major new experience or opportunity, you may go along with that kind of thing, but it doesn't sink in really. Mr. Rickey thought of it as preparatory, and I also felt Mr. Rickey was using it as a test. I think he really wanted to see how Jackie would react to provocation. I am a trainer myself, and we use role playing as a means of finding out if people are suitable for certain roles.

Rust: Well, let me tell you this, Rachael. My father and I were at Roosevelt Stadium that day when the Montreal Royals came in to play the Jersey City Giants, and—I mean, I had tears in my eyes. I didn't believe what I was seeing. I never thought it would work out. I mean I can't say I didn't think that black ballplayers didn't have the ability. I just never thought Arthur George Rust, Jr. would live to see it. And Jackie got four bingles that day. He hit a round tripper, stole two bases, and they beat the whey out of the Giants 14 to 1. What are your memories of that day?

Mrs. R: Oh, that was a staggering experience, because, remember, we had come up from the south. Jackie had had a bad spring training. He had been in a slump for a long time. As a matter of fact, we celebrated his first hit down there by having a special dinner. That's how bad things were. So, not only did he have this explosion of a wonderful day on all scores, but it was a relief. We never doubted that he could play, but we didn't know if he could play under the circumstances that he had to play under.

Rust: Rachael, he lost his hair. He almost had a breakdown. You got threats about kidnapping your youngster—and on and on.

Mrs. R: Well, you handle it in the context of what you believe is the larger goal. I think the reports about a near breakdown are exaggerated. Jackie had stress symptoms at the end of the Montreal season, and he couldn't eat for a week. He didn't feel like eating. He couldn't eat or sleep well, and we went to a doctor. The doctor said there is nothing wrong with you, but you are under a great deal of stress. Take a week off. And Jackie refused to take a week off. He took a day off and he felt much better. He recovered fully, and he went back into the season. So he didn't have a near breakdown, but by the time they were winning and he could afford to let his stress symptoms surface, he'd had them.

Rust: Were you satisfied by Ueberroth's gesture to put the number 42 on all second sacks throughout the leagues—on opening day at least?

Mrs. R: I am thrilled by Baseball Commissioner Peter Ueberroth's interest in doing more than that—that symbolic stuff. Peter Ueberroth declared 1987 to be a season dedicated to Jack. He talked about some substantial things. He knows that the structures in baseball need to be changed, and he talked about the lack of black managers, about not having blacks in the front offices and not having blacks in his own office. He also is co-chairing our endowment campaign with Bill Cosby. He said that he wants the foundation to live in perpetuity. Well, if he can do those kinds of things and give that kind of leadership, it is just as important to me as Rickey's role was in the early days.

Rust: What type of a relationship did Jackie have with the media when he came up, and how did it progress through his career?

Mrs. R: He had a mixed relationship with the media. There were sportswriters who would deliberately provoke him. Early on he had to take that along with the abuse at the ballparks. When he got his chance, he could answer them back and he was quite capable of managing that. There were also sportswriters who were very supportive of him, and he would take time or spend time with those who were more supportive of him, rather than those who were deliberately antagonizing him.

Rust: Was there a point in his career where he felt accepted by other players and managers, or did he never really feel totally accepted?

Mrs. R: He felt totally accepted. Well, totally is a rather comprehensive word. He felt a part of the team he was with when he really began to know his Dodger teammates, and I think he really felt very good about that. But he wrote in his own book that "I never had it made," meaning that there was still a lot to be done. Total acceptance is not something that he enjoyed, nor is it something that any of us can enjoy.

Rust: I guess that almost answers my next question. How do you feel that racial prejudices have worked themselves out from the time your husband started to work them out? Do you feel that it has reached the level where it should be more in the administrative part or do you feel that enough—not enough, obviously—but that a lot has been done?

Legends

Mrs. R: I think we have made progress in a number of areas, certainly in bringing black athletes into organized sports, not just baseball. We have done that, and that is to the advantage of the teams as well as to the individuals. Where we need to make a breakthrough is not only in management but in ownership. We have got to get into the system totally where it benefits us as well as the team. And right now it's kind of a one-way street. So I think there are a lot more changes to be made.

Rust: I have always heard that one of Jackie's real close friends on the ballclub was Peewee Reese. Was he one of the first guys who kinda took Jackie under his wing the first year or so?

Mrs. R: Yes, that is true. Jackie and Peewee had to form a combination, they had to pair up in terms of the work they had to do. It became imperative for them to do that, and I think that helped to foster the relationship. Peewee himself speaks about converting and being able—once he could recognize the need to—to respect Jack as a man.

Rust: Was Jackie the kind of man, say, who would bring the pressures from the ballpark home, and did he openly discuss what he should have done at the end of a particular ballgame?

Mrs. R: The interesting thing is that for twelve years— I'm exaggerating, it was ten years—I went to the ballpark with Jack. I went to work with him, and so I could see for myself what was happening. We would review the things that had happened on the way home, and by the time we reached the house we were really ready for our family. In some of the big issues where he was having big emotional reaction to things, yes, we had to talk about it at the dinner table. We tried to keep the children involved in what was happening, so that they could understand his moods and such and the kind of concerns that we had.

Rust: Will you correct me if I'm wrong, but I had always heard stories that Enos Slaughter and/or Dixie Walker got up a petition to have Jackie kicked off the ballclub after the then National League president Ford Frick stepped in.

Mrs. R: There was a petition. I don't know who started it. I don't know if anyone knows who started it, but we know who some of the participants were. The historical fact is that there was a petition. It was that form of opposition, and that form of opposition was dealt with. I think that is what we needed to remember, not so much who was there.

Rust: What gave Ebbets Field that certain aura, that mystique? Why was that particular ballpark in the entire era of New York so "different" in terms of the personalities, the Robinsons, the Campanellas, the Newcombes, as opposed to the New York Yankees team of that same era?

Mrs. R: Well, I think there are a number of factors. One is that it was such a small park, and it was a home-like atmosphere. You could walk around that ballpark and get to know sections of it.

Rust: Intimate?

Mrs. R: Very intimate. Then the park was taken through this so-called social experiment. That had to alert people to some of the things, the racism in our society and ways to combat it. We felt very comfortable in that park, and we *lived* in it—we lived in it and it was smaller. And then being the underdogs made it a uniting factor. The Yankees were the people who had it all, and we expected them to do nothing better than to win all the time.

Rust: Was there ever a time when Jackie just would come home and forget about baseball and the racial things and everything?

Legends

Mrs. R: Yes, we had a very rich home life, and baseball was not the all-consuming part of our lives. We had a child in the first year of our marriage, and two others subsequent to that. When we came home, we did what families do. We had fun together, we did special things together. We had to live by seasons, you know, and by the baseball schedules, but within those kinds of constraints, we had lots of things to do to relax and also to enjoy each other.

Rust: When the Dodgers traded Jackie to the Giants in December 1956 and then he retired, did he just make that decision alone? Or did he talk to you, like should he go— or did he just resent it? I know in his heart when the Dodgers and Giants played, you know, they hated each other.

Mrs. R: Yes, they were our enemies, for sure. He had started two years before he retired; he had started to get restless in baseball. He began to feel it was hard to get ready for spring training. He began to feel he had many other things he wanted to do. He was not one of those people who had to linger in the sport in order to have a meaningful life. During his winter season, traveling south and traveling west, he kind of knew about the problems around the country, so he was rather eager to get out. He was terribly disappointed by the trade. He didn't think they would ever trade him, and in particular, surely not to the Giants. But, no, he had signed a contract with Chock Full O' Nuts before he was traded—he just beat them to the punch.

Rust: A few years ago, Rachael, Vince Coleman of the St. Louis Cardinals was asked by a writer about Jackie Robinson, and he replied, "I don't know nothing about no Jackie Robinson." Weren't you very upset as I was?

Mrs. R: Well, I hesitate to say it, but I think I should say it. I think it becomes a statement that people are taking out of context. Sometimes ignorance gets displayed and people get taken off guard. I don't know what happened, and I don't know why he said it, or what the circumstances were. All black ballplayers do not pay tribute to Jack, but, there is a mix there. We have people who have different attitudes and different responses.

Rust: That was said after the tarpaulin ran over his head. Don't they realize, though, if it were not for Jackie—I mean, what this man went through. They would never ever be known—they would never have made it. I mean, how could they not recognize Jackie?

Mrs. R: You know what they want? They want to be recognized for their own effort, and they don't want it attributed to another person. They don't all have a sense of history.

Rust: Did Jackie do a lot of speaking and public appearances?

Mrs. R: Yes, he did quite a bit of speaking and going to small affairs, whether they were at schools or churches or synagogues. He was very interested in communicating with other people and very interested in having a platform to get some of his ideas across. And since he was very heavily focused on education, he really felt that if we could talk to each other and if we could examine things together, somehow things would get better. He took every opportunity to do that. I must say, there were times when he would get paid—not much, usually expenses. Very rarely did he get big speaking dates—very rarely. So he did it as a part of his overall mission. He did it sometimes at some personal sacrifice. It thrilled him to be able to do that. He was the kind of person who decided he would prepare for opportunities. He wasn't a great speaker when he finished with baseball, and he decided that he had to learn to speak. He wanted to get across some of his ideas. He used to work crossword puzzles in order to enlarge his vocabulary. And he would write all his own speeches and do many drafts of them, so he would get better at it, more fluent. I am not surprised that he did that. Believe me, he enjoyed it.

Rust: Did Jackie have political aspirations?

Mrs. R: No, I don't think he really ever had any political ambitions for himself. His feeling was that if he got people to be more active in the political arena, then we had to get behind the candidates. We had to get behind both black and white candidates so that some of the things that we needed were incorporated into their agendas. He never expressed any particular political ambition. He liked to feel that he was participating in promoting or supporting the candidate that he thought would do the most good. I think he had had enough of political life—I should say public life—not to want to get in, not to want to get locked into a political position. You know, there are certain constraints about politicians that he didn't have to deal with. He was able to be himself and not take the consequences in the sense that you would have to if you were a politician and had to be accountable to a party or to the voters.

Rust: Why did you move out of Brooklyn?

Mrs. R: (Laughter) That's a very good question. I don't think I have ever really thought of it as moving out of Brooklyn. Jack and I had both been raised in California, and we had always lived in a little house with a lawn around it. That's what we were looking for. So when we moved to Long Island, we bought such a house. We bought an old house.

Rust: Oh, on Long Island?

Mrs. R: Yes. We moved to St. Albans on 177th Street, and there we had a yard for the children to play in. We had a little more space. It was not moving away from Brooklyn, I can assure you. We loved Brooklyn—still do.

Rust: Let me ask you this. When Jackie dealt with Branch Rickey . . . Branch Rickey, I had heard, had a heart of gold, but kept it to himself. He was only tight with the money as far as that was concerned. I heard that he was a good person. I know when he met Jackie he took out the Bible. How did you and Jackie feel about that?

Mrs. R: We felt that he was a good man, that we were fortunate in coming along at a time when we could join forces with that kind of person. He was not a generous man as far as giving money was concerned, and there was no real room for negotiations. That was the other thing about baseball in those days. I mean, it was a real plantation system. You took what they gave you and you went where they told you to go. Contrast that with today. It is really kind of amazing where this sport has moved, but definitely Mr. Rickey was a shrewd businessman and that did not take away from his interest in and concern for the social issue.

Rust: What was the emotion felt by you and Jackie during his signing with the Dodgers. And what was it like seeing him on the field for the first time.

Mrs. R: Well, I think you can imagine that . . . Remember, we were in our early twenties and we had come east for the first time from California. We were here without family or friends. The excitement was just overpowering, and I think the excitement took away the sting of things that were going wrong. The pain of separation from our families, or the concern we had about establishing a new life as a newly-married couple. So that we really joined up and paired up as partners, and it was exhilarating—it really was. Even some of the troublesome things—we felt we were kind of a powerful pair, that we could deal with them.

Legends

Rust: Rachael, let's divvy up these signings. Let's talk about the first signing with the Montreal ballclub in October 1945, and then differentiate that with the signing with the big club in April of '46. Let's take Montreal in '45—what was the feeling?

Mrs. R: I think the feeling in '45 was that it was a trial. Nothing was guaranteed, nothing certain. Exciting, of course, but if you didn't get out of the minor leagues, you hadn't made it. Having had a successful year and having proved one's ability to play in the majors, the second signing was much more of an acclamation of one's self. Yes, I can do it—I can do it in terms of my skills; I can do it in terms of handling the social situations that I will encounter. So you move into that area. It shows a lot more confidence and a lot more feeling that you *know* that you can do it— you can make a contribution to the team, and it doesn't have all the scary elements of failure.

Rust: All right—in '47—Robbie with the big club—July 5 of '47, Larry Doby with the Cleveland Indians—July 17, Willard Brown and Hank Thompson with the St. Louis Browns. Bankhead joins the Dodgers in August of that year. First time he played he hit a ball up into the seats. I'll never forget that one. Did Jack talk to these guys? Did he speak to Larry? Did he talk to Larry? Did he talk to Willard? Did they communicate?

Mrs. R: Believe me, he did. He would find ways of communicating with them. He was a competitor in terms of the game, but in terms of his aspirations for black people, he was not competitive. He not only talked to them and tried to help and encourage them, but he even scouted some of them. He went barnstorming through the south looking for the raw talent and talking about being affirmed. You're really affirmed not by being the first but by having the second and third and fourth coming into the arena. It tells you that there is a real impact and that there will be change. He felt thrilled by the entry of the other players.

Rust: Rachael, what kind of reception did you and Jackie receive in Montreal in 1946?

Mrs. R: I would love to talk about Montreal because it was such a special experience. Remember, we had come up from the south and he had some real problems there in terms of the laws that related to segregation. So by the time we hit Montreal, we were expecting almost anything. We didn't know just what to expect. My first encounter with Canadians was looking for an apartment. Now, if you are black and you are looking for housing, you always expect the worst. I mean, it was—there is just an instinctive feeling that you are going to be rejected or you are going to have a hard time. When someone opened the door to an apartment where I wanted to rent, and she smiled at me and invited me in and didn't do a double take, or didn't, you know, put her foot in the door . . . invited me in to sit down, and she prepared tea. She asked me if I liked the apartment. It was a small apartment, but lovely. I said I liked it and I would like to take it. She said "I'm going to leave all of my things for you to use," and she left me all her linens and china and that sort of thing. I felt that I had recovered my dignity—the dignity that I had lost when I was in the south and had been treated in ways that were kind of subhuman. That good experience persisted throughout our time in Montreal. Even though we were living in a French Canadian neighborhood where we couldn't communicate with the neighbors nor they with us, a spirit developed between us —a spirit of cooperation and collaboration and respect that I carry with me throughout my life. I think it was the ideal launching point for us, because I was not experienced; we had new confidence and new feelings of self-esteem that we could take back into the American scene where things weren't always that good.

Rust: What players on the Montreal teams did you feel really helped Jackie?

Mrs. R: On that team I can't really single out a player that I thought was especially helpful—I am still in touch with Jean-Pierre Roy and we talk about the old days and his feelings. Right at this moment he is developing a group called "The Friends of Jackie Robinson."

Rust: The last year that Jackie was in the majors was 1956. What impressions do you have of that year?

Mrs. R: Well, we had won in 1955. We had finally won a World Series, and we were the champs. That had a lot to do with the way we felt about ourselves in 1956. We were happy that Jack had had such opportunity to participate in that. We also went to Japan as a team and had a chance to see how the Japanese related to the American ballplayers. It was a good culminating year, and I think Jack was glad to get out of baseball. I was a Jackie Robinson fan, and I really was going to miss him in baseball, to tell you the truth. I deferred to his judgment, but I hated to see him quit . . .

Rust: Rachael, Jackie gave off a certain aura—the feeling that he knew what he was doing, and he took a great deal of pride in it.

Mrs. R: Yes, he did. That came across in his stance and in the way he carried himself and in the way he presented himself to the world. I saw that in him when we were students at UCLA. He was a man who was proud of his identity. He didn't have the ambivalence that some others had. He could deal with it in a positive way, so it always came through in terms of his presentation of himself. I think we all need models. If we don't pattern ourselves after someone, at least we need living models that say it can be done. I know that Jackie was a role model for many people.

Rust: I have always felt that Jackie's joining the Dodgers in 1947 set the stage for Montgomery and then the later events in the 1960s. I have always felt that he has been certainly, if not the greatest, then one of the greatest civil rights leaders that we have had.

Mrs. R: Yes, I agree with you.

Rust: Let me just ask you about the first couple of years when Jackie was under orders from Branch Rickey to be passive—to be passive in the field—obviously that wasn't his personality. . . .

Mrs. R: No.

Rust: How was he able to control himself?

Mrs. R: He made an agreement that had some major significance, so it was worth the effort that he put into it. It was a totally unnatural experience for him. This is a man who reacted quickly to injustices, and not with a chip on his shoulder but kind of a readiness to tackle things. It was difficult for him to restrain himself. He was not the exciting ballplayer then that he became once he could totally be himself—once he could not only engage in the game the way the other players did but could use the avenues of protest that they used and feel energized by the annoyances and anger that he felt rather than be depressed by them.

Rust: I've read where Jackie was really never one of Walter O'Malley's favorites. Was there something that conflicted within their personalities, or was it just the fact that Jackie was so close with Branch Rickey?

Mrs. R: I think it was the latter; I don't think it was a personality conflict so much as that he was a Rickey man. His primary loyalty had been and continued to be to Rickey.

In the new administration they weren't doing things the way Rickey did, and they didn't have the same feelings. They hadn't gone through the same things and experiences together. I think that created the tension. I don't necessarily think it was so much in the personality.

Rust: Why didn't you and Jackie ever live in Harlem?

Mrs. R: No, we never lived in Harlem. We lived in Brooklyn, and we lived in St. Albans, and then we moved up to Connecticut. Jack and I both worked in Harlem a great deal, and, as you know, Jack started the Freedom National Bank in Harlem. He was very connected to it, and he was also very connected to the Harlem YMCA at 135th Street. He used to go up there to play with the kids and shoot baskets and try to make contact with them. So we felt very close to Harlem, and I still do.

Rust: Rachael, let's talk about the Foundation and how people can contribute.

Mrs. R: There are two ways, and we certainly need funds; we are building an endowment campaign right now because nonprofits have been living hand-to-mouth, and we are no exception. We have decided that we are going to be around in the twenty-third century. We decided to just skip over century twenty-one and twenty-two because I really want to see this organization live in perpetuity. Therefore, we would be happy to receive funds at 80 Eighth Avenue, New York, NY 10011, and in any amount and at any time.

Rust: Rachael, any time I talk about Joseph Paul Di-Maggio, Red Barber, Joe Louis, Nat King Cole, and Jack Roosevelt Robinson, I get all choked up. Rachael, thanks for talking with me.

Mrs. R: Oh, it's been wonderful—and I do thank you.

8

Richie Ashburn

A H, Richie Ashburn. One of the best leadoff hitters I ever saw. He could really get on base. He received a lot of walks, ran like the wind, and could bunt and beat out a lot of hits. Ashburn was a choke-grip type of hitter. He just excelled at punching the ball to left field. The man covered as much ground as anyone I ever saw. And, personally, I always found him to be forth-right, particularly in his treatment of Jackie Robinson when he was playing under manager Ben Chapman. Richie didn't skirt the issue of his poor treatment of Robinson. He said that was the thing to do then. He said he was only following orders.

Rust: Despite your skills as a hitter, a runner, and a fielder, the play for which you are most remembered was a thrill. Without it, there would have been no Dick Sisler round-tripper in that 10th inning to win the 1950 pennant. Tell me about it. You nailed Cal Abrams at the plate. Let's talk about that.

Legends

Ashburn: Well, okay. It was an important throw, obviously, but it was nowhere near the best that I ever made. It was really kind of a routine play at a very important time. It was a play that, you know, you practice on and practice on. And it just came up and I made the good throw, but it was really kind of a routine play at a rather crucial time.

Rust: He was out by about fifteen feet as I recall.

Ashburn: In fact, the catcher, Stan Lopata had time to catch the ball and then run up towards the third-base line, towards the runner, to meet him. Art, when you're thrown out that far, somebody's made a mistake, and that was the third-base coach, Milt Stock. As I remember, I think he got fired because of that.

Rust: That's right—Stock never came back. All right, I recall reading about you in the *Sporting News* when I was about sixteen years old. I think we're both about the same age—you had gone to a St. Louis Cardinals tryout camp in 1943. What happened?

Ashburn: I went to the camp and I was still too young to sign. I wasn't even out of high school. A year or two later, the Cardinals offered me a bonus of—oh, I don't know, I think it was $2,500 or something—which was quite a bit.

Rust: It was a lot of money then.

Ashburn: It was a lot of money in 1944—and 1945—and, it was a lot of money for the Cardinals, because they didn't give bonuses. I believe Branch Rickey was running that organization then, and, you know, he wasn't throwing much money around. It was a compliment that they even offered me a bonus. I was offered a small bonus by the Yankee organization. It's kind of ironic that Branch Rickey was running the Dodgers in 1945. I went to Brooklyn for a tryout. I was a catcher then. Branch Rickey, who was acknowledged

110

as maybe the greatest judge of baseball talent who ever lived, told me at that time that I should go back to Nebraska and do what I was going to do. He said I'd never be a major league baseball player. Now he was in Brooklyn then, and he had not scouted me in that Cardinal tryout camp. Really, another scout by the name of Joe McDermott was running that camp then, but the first time that Branch Rickey actually ever saw me play he told me to quit.

Rust: I'm glad you didn't listen to him. All right, in 1948—I think that's when you joined the Phillies—you replaced Harry "The Hat" Walker.

Ashburn: Yes. That's right. And he had just won the batting title in 1947, and I think he hit .363.

Rust: Something in that neighborhood. Now tell us about the Whiz Kids, the 1950 bunch. You finished sensationally the latter part of 1949. Did you guys have any idea that you'd romp to the National League pennant in 1950?

Ashburn: Well, we didn't romp, but we did win it. In 1949 we were a good club. We were very young, and I think at the end of the season we were probably the best team in the league. In fact, our manager, Eddie Sawyer, after the last game was played in that 1949 season, had a very short meeting. He wasn't very much for meetings, but he had a short meeting and he said, "Come on back next year. We're going to win it. Be ready to win." We finished third in 1949, but we were coming on fast and so it was no great surprise that we at least thought we could win.

Rust: I'll throw some of the names across of the Whiz Kids. Let's start on the mound. When I say Robin Roberts, what do you think of?

Ashburn: He's the best pitcher I ever played with, certainly. No doubt in my mind, the greatest competitor I ever played with in terms of pitching. He was one of those once-in-a-lifetime pitchers that come along. I have played against probably better pitchers than even Robin—I'm thinking of a Juan Marichal or a Bob Gibson or a Sandy Koufax—but over the long haul, I think that probably Robin pitched better than all of them in terms of total wins.

Rust: What about Curt Simmons?

Ashburn: Curt was an outstanding pitcher. If Curt Simmons had not gone into the Army and if Curt Simmons had not cut off part of his big toe with the lawn mower, Curt Simmons might have been greater than Roberts. When Curt came up, he threw the ball as hard as anybody I have ever seen. He not only threw hard, but his ball had tremendous movement. I think it was Stan Musial in a book he wrote with Bob Broeg years ago that cited Simmons as the toughest pitcher that he ever faced. And, you know, that's quite a compliment from a great hitter. But Curt had a very deceiving delivery. He had tremendous velocity, and, as I said, he had a lot of movement on the ball. He was a very good athlete.

Rust: What about Jim Konstanty—he played in 74 games and had about 22 saves that year. And I think Eddie Sawyer—I mean, your staff, was so damn tired that he had to start in the World Series.

Ashburn: That's right. He started the first game of the World Series against the Yankees. He lost it 1 to 0, so he pitched a great game.

Rust: Raschi—Vic Raschi beat him in that one.

Ashburn: Yeah. Konstanty was a character in some respects. He was older. He was one of the older players on our team. He thought he could get anybody out that ever walked up to home plate. What he had—he had pinpoint control with two pitches, a little slider and a palm ball. And he just—he had more confidence in himself than anybody I have ever seen for not having that much reason to have confidence in himself. But he did, and he thought if a hitter got a hit off of him, it was—he never gave any credit to the hitter, it was always something that he must have done wrong.

Rust: In the World Series, you played the Yankees tough —I've forgotten, I think the Yankees sent Raschi in the first game. I think it was The Chief, Reynolds, in the second; I think Steady Eddie Lopat beat you; and then Whitey Ford. What did you think about when you saw Whitey Ford for the first time?

Ashburn: I thought this guy is going to be a great pitcher. I mean, he became a Hall of Famer. When I first saw him, he was a rookie and he could throw pretty hard. He was never a guy that blew you right out of there, but he threw harder earlier in his career. He had a better fast ball, and then later on when he lost a little of that fast ball, he became a breaking ball pitcher with tremendous control. And he knew how to pitch. He knew the strengths and weaknesses of the hitters.

Rust: All right. Your last year in the "bigs" was in 1962. You played with the Mets at the late-lamented Polo Grounds. Do you want to talk about that? How was that last year with that ball club under Casey Stengel?

Ashburn: It was about what I expected in some ways. I knew we weren't going to have, you know, a very good team. We had players who, at some point in their careers, were outstanding players, but they were towards the end of their careers. I didn't think it would be as bad as it was. I have always felt about that year that I wouldn't go through it again for anything, but, on the other hand, I wouldn't have missed it for anything. Because there were a lot of positive things, you know, that came up in that year for me in baseball.

Rust: Elaborate on that—what positive things?

Ashburn: Well, one positive thing was the support of the New York fans. It's the only year that I have ever been involved in where nobody ever expected you to win and there was absolutely no pressure on you to win. But the fans not only came out, they were generally very supportive. I saw something happen during that season that was a revelation to me, and that was kind of nice. When the Giants and Dodgers, who had moved to the West Coast, of course, came back to the Polo Grounds, the old Giant fans and the old Dodger fans, a lot of them came out early in the season and were rooting for the old Giants and the old Dodgers. Well, that changed. It was a perceptible change that started somewhere in the middle of the season, and the fans, I don't know how they felt about it, but it appeared that they thought, "the heck with these guys who moved out of this city, we're going to root for our own team." And I saw that change in the fans. And of course Mets fans—the Mets have had a tremendous following ever since.

Rust: Richie, explain the situation when you spiked Jackie Robinson.

Ashburn: Well, I did spike Jackie and at the time I probably did it deliberately. I'm from the midwest and I don't know nothing or didn't know nothing from anything. All I knew was that at the time it seemed to be the thing to do on our ballclub—to try to hurt him. Well, I learned after I did hurt him I was very sorry about it, and I told him about that later.

Rust: Well, you know, you took the question right out of my mouth. I was just going to ask how did you feel when you realized that you were fighting a man who practically had his hands tied behind his back. You know, he was a great competitor and he was a great fighter. How about any of your teammates? Did they ever respond that way?

Ashburn: Not that I know of.

Rust: You had a manager from Alabama by the name of Chapman, right? Ben Chapman.

Ashburn: I know he got on Jackie a lot. I also saw a game in Philadelphia one day where he walked over to our dugout. This was after our dugout, including our manager, had been all over him, and Jackie said to Ben Chapman—he said, "Okay, buddy, let's see how tough you are. You and me will go at it right here." Look, I have always admired him as a baseball player. I admired him from the first day that I saw him as a baseball player. Of all the great players on that Dodger team in the early fifties, which is the best team I have ever seen put together, he is the guy who hurt us the most. We used to knock him down almost every time he came up to home plate. We'd try to hit him hard on double plays. It was terrible, the things he had to go through. But every time we knocked him down, he got up and he hit a line drive somewhere. And I said to our players one day, "Maybe we ought to stop knocking this guy down, he's killing us."

Then later on, things let up on Jackie. You said something that I have always said about him. He was a very fierce competitor on the ballfield. I got to know him a little better after that, and I got to know his wife who was, and still is, a great lady.

Rust: Richie, your memories of the Robinson performance in that final day of 1951 against your ballclub?

Ashburn: Well, he saved the game with a great play in the bottom of the ninth inning back of second base.

Rust: That's right, knocking himself out doing it.

Ashburn: Yeah. He was down for awhile. It took a while for the game to resume. I remember that. He made a tremendous play and then, of course, he beat us in the fourteenth inning with a home run. That was Jackie. I mean, he was just—he was just a magnificient ballplayer.

Rust: How do you like being a broadcaster, Richie?

Ashburn: Well, I tell you—I've just finished my twenty-fourth year at it, and it's a job that I originally turned down. To be honest with you, I didn't think I wanted to do it. But after I retired as a player, these people in Philadelphia came to me in Nebraska. I lived out there and they said, "Would you like this job?" I said, "No," and they said, "Well, we've got three months before the season starts. Think about it for awhile and then let us know." So I decided to take it, and here I am.

Rust: Richie, tell us about Casey, about Stengelese?

Ashburn: Hey, we could understand him most of the time. I think that most of the approach that he had was for the benefit of the media. I will admit there were times he said some things that I didn't understand at first, but I would figure them out after a while. The first thing I ever heard him yell was in spring training. He kept yelling at the hitters. He kept yelling "Butcher Boy, Butcher Boy." It took a little while for us to figure that out, but that was . . . he wanted the hitter to meet the ball and he associated "meat" with butchers, and so—you know, those were the connections you had to finally make on some of those things.

He could be very confusing. He was the reason—the big reason that I would not have missed that '62 season for anything. He was a very, very nice man. I found out also he was a pretty good manager. It's hard to tell if a guy could manage when you're behind five or six runs in every single ballgame. You know, there isn't very much a manager can do but just sit there.

Rust: Let me tell you a Casey Stengel story from the media point of view. In 1969, I was on NBC Television. I was interviewing him after the Mets had beaten Baltimore and I remember him standing on the table and I remember asking him how did they do it. And he said, "Vodka. They were drinking vodka." And I said to myself, What the hell is he talking about?—What I wanted to ask you, Richie, what did you think of who I think to be the quintessential ballplayer, Joseph Paul DiMaggio?

Ashburn: I could see what everybody got excited about. You know, I've gotten to know Joe since he retired, and through the years I've been to different things with him. And I tell you what has impressed me more about him than anything is that when you look up his record and see what he did, and then when you are around him, he never talks about it. He never says a word about it.

Rust: No, he doesn't. He won't.

Ashburn: You know, this guy, I think one year he struck out twenty times. My God, we have players now who do that in a week. Can you imagine a hitter like that with the lifetime average he had, .325, striking out twenty times a year—twenty-five times a year. I mean, you know, that's incredible.

Rust: Now my question is, in today's era we hear often about how today's athletes would do in the past and how the past athletes might do in today's game of baseball. In your opinion, with today's travel being more involved than it ever has been, what do you think the effect is, compared to when you played?

Legends

Ashburn: I don't think the travel is that big a deal. I traveled when I first came to the major leagues, and we traveled mostly by train. We didn't have the coast-to-coast travel or flights or things like that. I don't think that travel has that much to do with it. But, you're talking about . . . your question about players today against players of the past—that's a tough one. You know, I've seen players, and I've played with and against players that could play in anybody's generation. There are players today that that's true of. I think the one difference is that there are as many good players today, and maybe more. But there are a lot more bad players, and I think that's probably because of the expansion. You see, there used to be sixteen teams in the major leagues— now there are twenty-six.

Rust: Kind of watered down, eh, Rich?

Ashburn: It's almost doubled. You know, I don't see any Joe DiMaggios around today. I don't see any Stan Musials. I don't see any Willie Mayses. I don't see Roberto Clementes.

Rust: Now listen, Don Mattingly ain't exactly chopped liver, is he, Richie?

Ashburn: I don't get much opportunity to see Don play. We're talking about great ballplayers who could play in anybody's ballpark.

Rust: Richie, what are your parting thoughts on major league baseball today—you say the product is watered down—you don't think the ballplayers today are as great as the ballplayers in your time—you don't think much of Don Mattingly and Wade Boggs and Dave Winfield and Mike Schmidt. What are we talking about?

Ashburn: Well, first of all, I didn't say that, Art. Sure, there are great players today. I say there are great players today, and probably more. But there are also more bad players. I mean, look at the guys who stay in the league hitting .200 or even below that. You know, this completely baffles me. There are certainly a lot of clunkers up there, too.

Rust: Well, they had clunkers in your time, too, Richard.

Ashburn: Listen, we didn't have clunkers like they have today.

Rust: Well, there are a couple of guys in the Hall of Fame now who needed to DH back in your day.

Ashburn: Who's that?

Rust: I'm not going to name names, but you know who they are. Some of them couldn't catch a baseball in their gloves if you put it in their gloves, but they could hit it.

Ashburn: Well, but I'm not talking about guys in the league now who cannot hit or do anything. If you got a hitter in the Hall of Fame who couldn't field the ball, he must have been a hell of a hitter.

Rust: His initials are Ralph Kiner, for starters. Ralph probably won't talk to me anymore, but that's the way it is.

9

Don
Newcombe

WHEN you say Don New-
combe to me, I think of the first game of the 1949 World
Series. Newcombe, the Dodgers' black freshman hurler,
and "Chief" Allie Reynolds kept a capacity crowd at the
Big Ball Orchard in the South Bronx on the edge of their
seats as they dueled 0-0 throughout.

Newcombe pitched like an old pro, as if he had par-
ticipated in the World Series before. His fastball was hopping and his curve broke sharply. As the ballplayers would
say, he was throwing aspirin tablets. The Yankee bats were
swinging at air. And Reynolds was equally superb. After eight
innings, Newk had eleven Ks. He was just two away from
the Series record of thirteen strikeouts set in 1929 by Athletics' right-hander Howard Ehmke. Newcombe didn't allow a walk and gave up only four hits to the Bronx Bombers.

In the ninth inning, Tommy Henrich led off for the
Yankees. The great clutch-hitter, nicknamed "Old Relia-
ble," was facing a top fastball artist. Newcombe worked
him carefully, throwing two balls low and away to the pull
hitter. The third pitch to Henrich was a low curve. Henrich
timed it perfectly and jerked it into the right-field stands
for a heartbreaking, 1-0 Yankee victory. Big Don never
looked back. He knew it was gone. He just tucked his glove
in his back pocket and walked off the field.

Don Newcombe

He was a no-nonsense guy. A bit irascible from time to time but, deep down, very introverted. He concealed that with an attitude. But he was a fun-loving guy. I always thought he was a courageous guy who could overcome anything. And he proved that in his winning bout with alcohol.

Rust: Donny, you know, when you say Don Newcombe to Arthur George, I go back to 1949, first game of the 1949 World Series. You against the Chief, Allie Reynolds. Your fast ball was hopping. Your curve ball was dropping off the table. You and the Chief, Reynolds, were throwing very, very small baseballs. I believe you didn't walk anybody and gave up only about four bingles to a real big apple-knocking Yankee ballclub, with Yogi Berra, Joseph Paul DiMaggio, Hank Bauer. Bottom of the ninth, Tommy Henrich, two balls, low and away—and then, what happened?

Newcombe: That's history. Tommy Henrich hit a home run!

Rust: What are your memories of that particular ballgame?

Newcombe: I remember throwing the pitch and walking off the mound.

Rust: You never looked back. You never even looked.

Newcombe: I never even turned around. I knew it was gone. I had thrown enough of them in my life up to that point, Art, I knew it was gone, and us pitchers, most of 'em do. It is just a reflex thing to turn around and watch it. I watched a lot of them in my career to see how far they would go, but I knew they were gone when they left the bat. And when Tommy hit that ball that day, I knew it was gone, so there was no need to turn around. I just put my glove in my pocket and went on off the field and into the clubhouse.

Rust: Don, you were the first black pitcher in a World Series game actually to pitch. What were your feelings that day?

Newcombe: I guess I had a modicum of fear, I guess you could call it, about the vaunted Yankee Dynasty that was putting the fear in everybody in the American League that year. And here I was, a rookie being give a chance—given a chance to make a history, to be the first black man to pitch in a World Series game against the New York Yankees. But when I started warming up, I didn't feel that fear. With Jackie Robinson and Roy Campanella being there, they just said, go out and throw it, big fella. Let's see what happens. And that's what I did.

Rust: I saw you during World War II. I think it was in 1943 with the Newark Eagles. You worked for Mr. and Mrs. Abe Manley. What are your memories of that time, playing with the Eagles in the Negro National League?

Newcombe: Well, I was 17 years old when I started with the Newark Eagles. That was in 1944, Art, and I had no idea in my wildest dreams that five years later I would be pitching in the Yankee Stadium against the New York Yankees. There was no way that a kid from the ghetto in Elizabeth, New Jersey, could ever think along those lines. My thoughts never went along those lines. In fact, Art, I never had a baseball idol. I never had a baseball idol, other than Satchel Paige, and there I was playing against him. I never had a Joe DiMaggio or a Hank Greenberg, or one of those players in organized baseball as an idol.

Rust: Was that for ethnic reasons?

Newcombe: It was just something that never entered my thoughts. We went out there . . . the way it was going, it was never going to be ... so what would be the use of idolizing them at 17 years old?

Rust: I can understand the frustration, because I went through the same damn thing. In October '45, I saw you at Ebbets Field. It was an All-Star game. One team, of course, composed of Negro National League All-Stars, and on the other team were major leaguers. If my memory serves me correct, I saw George "Whitey" Kurowski; I saw Frank McCormick, the Reds' first sacker; I saw Eddie Stanky; I saw Buddy Kerr; I saw Ralph Branca. I understand that was the pivotal game for Don Newcombe in major league baseball.

Newcombe: Yes, I started that game at Ebbets Field that day in the rain. And, as you recall, and I know you do, how cold it was. . . .

Rust: Yeah, cold as hell.

Newcombe: And it was raining that day, and we wanted to play because we had 10,000 in the stands and most of them were black folks. They had beaten us the first two games. Ralph Branca had shut us out in Newark on a Friday night, and then they had beaten us. We wanted to play the game because we had a chance to make a few bucks.

I started the game and I was doing pretty well against that major league all-star team, but I hurt my arm in the third inning. I was taken out of the game and went into the clubhouse, and I sat there by myself and I began to cry. I thought my baseball career was all over. I was only 18 years old, and I guess you can understand my trepidation, worrying and wondering about my career. And into the clubhouse walked a white man named Clyde Sukeforth. He was then at the time the chief scout for the Brooklyn Dodgers. I didn't know it then. Into the clubhouse walked this big man with this great big hat on. I never saw such a big hat in my whole life on such a small man . . . and he asked me if my name was Don Newcombe, and I said, "Yes," and he said, "What are you crying about?" and I said, "Well, I just hurt my arm out there in the game, and I guess my career is over."

And he said, "What makes you think that?" Then he said, "I'm Clyde Sukeforth, and I'm with the Dodgers and Mr. Branch Rickey, who owns the Dodgers." I said, "Who's Mr. Rickey?" I didn't even know who he was, Art, to be honest with you. Well, he said, "He's the owner of the Dodgers, and he is thinking of starting a Negro team to play at Ebbets Field while the white team is on the road. They're going to be called the Brown Dodgers." He said he's got a few other players under contract who happen to be black, and he wanted to know if I would be interested in talking to Mr. Rickey about this possibility.

And I said, "Sure, if he is going to pay me some money," and he said, "Sure." And he said, "Why don't you come over to Ebbets Field. Come over to Montague Street, to the Dodger home office and talk to Mr. Rickey tomorrow morning." We're talking now on a Sunday afternoon in Ebbets Field. The next morning he wanted me to come to Mr. Rickey's office. And I did that. I came over from Newark, New Jersey, where I was staying at the time. And I spoke to Mr. Rickey, and he signed me to a contract.

Rust: I think Campy told me that you and he were assigned—they *wanted* to assign you to Danville in the Three-I League, and you were rejected. They didn't want any black ballplayers.

Newcombe: Yes, the president of the league said, "We don't want any . . . ," and I'm not going to use the word he used because everybody knows what that word is. . . .

Rust: It begins with an "N."

Don Newcombe

Newcombe: Right. "We don't want any of them out here
. . . if you send any of them out here, we're going to close
the league down."

Rust: So after that you went to Nashua and played under
Walter Alston?

Newcombe: Mr. Rickey called Buzzie Bavasi, who had the
Dodger team in Nashua, New Hampshire. That was the
only Dodger team that Roy Campanella and Don Newcombe could have played on. You see, they had no other
team in the lower classification. The higher classifications
were all in the South or in the West where they didn't want
the blacks in the first place. Mr. Rickey called Buzzie, who
was the general manager, on the phone, and he asked him
if he would take these two Negro players on his team. And
Buzzie wanted to know if we could play baseball. Mr. Rickey
said, "I think so, because I've signed them to contracts."
Buzzie said, "Send them up; we don't care what color they
are." And, Art, I want to add this, I wonder if Buzzie had
turned us down, or if Walter Alston had turned us down
. . . I wonder if you would ever have seen Roy Campanella
and Don Newcombe play professional baseball. I wonder
about that sometimes.

Rust: How would you describe that season at Nashua?
Playing under a Walter Alston? How was the treatment in
that town?

Newcombe: Oh, we had a wonderful time. The people
treated us well. Roy Campanella and I got . . . each time you
hit a home run, you got 100 chickens. I think Roy got 1,300
chickens—little baby chicks, which he sent home to Philadelphia to his Dad to raise for him. I got one or two or three
hundred, something like that. I gave them to Roy because I
had no place to have them raised. And we had a joyous time.
I was even their bus driver. We had a lot of fun there.

Legends

Rust: This is 1947, right off the top of my head. In '47 you went down to Caracas, Venezuela. And I think your manager there was Roy Campanella. Tell me about that.

Newcombe: That was a pretty nice season . . . playing for my roommate and my teammate, Roy Campanella, down in Venezuela. I pitched in a championship game, or it was the game that had we won it, we would have won the championship. I think I was wilder that day than I have ever been in my baseball career, Art. I mean, I walked eight or nine men. I think we lost the game 4-3. Roy was very, very disappointed because I was so wild that day, but, otherwise, we had a wonderful time, a wonderful season down there. Luke Easter was down there that year. He joined the Cleveland Indians two years later.

Rust: Ah, he could hit that baseball.

Newcombe: Harry "Suitcase" Simpson, myself, and John Rice. Roy, and Vernal Mathes, and quite a few of us were down there that year who happened to be black baseball players.

Rust: All right, so now, in '48 you go to the Montreal Royals in the International League, and Campy went to St. Paul in the American Association, right?

Newcombe: Yes.

Rust: All right, let's talk about Montreal.

Newcombe: It took some doing to get me to Montreal. I was very upset that I wasn't brought up to the Dodgers after that year I had in Nashua. I was 19-6 that second year in Nashua in 1947, and then after having a pretty good year in Venezuela, I was 7-4 down there. I didn't like the way I was being treated. And I had some problems with Mr. Rickey about that and also with his son, Branch, Junior. But then I finally got to the Montreal team and I had a pretty good year. I think I was 17-8 that year; we won the championship by about, oh, 10-12 games, I think. We had players on the team like Chuck Connors, Al Gionfrido, Bobby Morgan, and Sam Jethro, and players like that. We had a pretty good team.

Rust: What part did Jackie Roosevelt Robinson play in it? Did you talk with Jackie when you were having this difficulty?

Newcombe: Oh, yes, there were constant telephone calls to Jackie. But there weren't major problems, at least not racial problems. Sam Jethro and I were doing pretty good in Montreal, and Jackie and Roy had been in baseball for two years, almost going on three years. A lot of the problems had been solved to a degree. There wasn't that outward racism that Jackie and Roy experienced. So I didn't have to worry about it too much, along with Sam Jethro.

Rust: All right, your first year you win the National League Rookie of the Year Award. Talk about your first year with the Dodgers.

Newcombe: I went back to Montreal after pitching some pretty good games against the Dodgers. I was sent back to Montreal and I didn't understand that, so I jumped the club and went home.

Rust: I remember that.

Newcombe: I left spring training and went home, because I was terribly disappointed. After pitching a pretty good game against the Dodgers in spring training, I wasn't brought up to the Dodgers. I didn't understand what Mr. Rickey was doing, Art. There was a stairstep plan, a stairstep procedure that Mr. Rickey was adhering to—and there wasn't any guy by the name of Don Newcombe going to change that. He wanted Jackie first and then Roy, although in the interim he had bought Dan Bankhead up, if you remember, during the '47 season . . .

Rust: Yeah. It was in August of '47.

Newcombe: But as far as I was concerned, I was going to be brought up when and if the time arose. He wanted Jackie firmly entrenched, he wanted Roy firmly entrenched, and then if there was a need for me, he would bring me up. I didn't know that, and I just jumped the club and went home. I stayed home three days and then called Buzzie Bavasi back at Montreal and asked him if he would take a damn fool back on his ballclub. I was sorry. I had made a mistake. And he said if that damn fool can come back and win me 20 games, just send him back here. I went back to Montreal and started the season and pitched two good games. The first two games I think I pitched a shutout and a one-run game against the Newark Bears and some other team, and then I lost the next two games by one run, but they were four pretty good baseball games. Then I really thought that I should have been brought up to the Dodgers.

I began to get down on myself and I didn't understand what was going on. I wish to God I could have understood, but I didn't. I got pretty much down on myself, and then one day, about the fifteenth of May, Buzzie Bavasi called me into his office at Montreal. I got in my car and drove down to his ballpark, and Buzzie said to me, "How long will it take you to get home and get your wife back home and then meet Mr. Rickey at Roosevelt Field in Long Island . . . to fly to Chicago to join the Dodgers?" I said, "You're crazy, you're kidding me." I drove my car home from Montreal to Elizabeth, New Jersey, where I lived and then, the following day or two days later, I had to meet Mr. Rickey over at Roosevelt Field to join the Dodgers. We had to fly his plane out. We had to stop at Harrisburg, Pennsylvania,

128

to pick up Billy Cox, who they had just traded for, and then meet the big club in Chicago. I thought that was the happiest day of my life. And the happiest day was when I walked into that hotel and went into Jackie and Roy's room, and there they were, sitting there and having dinner. I said, here I am, part of the team with Jackie and Roy. I was never more happy in my life!

Rust: All right.

Newcombe: And then to get on the bus the next day and go to the baseball game at Wrigley Field. And they gave me number 36 with "DODGERS" written across the chest. I thought I was the biggest guy in the world.

Rust: All right, Newk, let's—again you say Newcombe to me and I think about '49. I think about the Chief. I think about Tommy Henrich. But I was at that playoff game. I call it the Bobby Thomson Game in October '51, at that bathtub, that green bathtub called the Polo Grounds. You were throwing very, very small baseballs for eight innings against the Giants. What happened? You were getting tired, obviously.

Newcombe: Well, if you recall, the Giants got a couple of squib hits. Alvin Dark and Don Mueller got squib hits. And then Whitey Lockman got an opposite field hit. I was still throwing the ball good.

Rust: But you were getting a little bit tired then, Don. I recall, from about the seventh inning you started aiming the ball. . . .

Newcombe: Well, Art, if you recall anything, you know I was throwing pretty hard. I think I struck out two of the three hitters that I faced in that inning. Leo Durocher has said in the ensuing years, "I wouldn't have taken Don Newcombe out. I would have taken Rube Walker, the catcher, out, and brought Roy Campanella in to catch that ninth inning." But that was his contention about what should have gone on. But when that meeting was held after Don Mueller broke his ankle sliding into third base . . .

Rust: And Hartung pinch-ran for him . . .

Newcombe: There was a meeting at the mound, and Jackie, Roy, and—not Roy, but Jackie, and Peewee, and Gil Hodges, and myself, and Charlie Dressen, the manager. Charlie Dressen said to Peewee Reese, "What do you guys think? This is your money as well as it is mine. What do you think we ought to do?" And Peewee said to him, I will always remember his words . . . he said, "Look, this is the guy who gave us his all and he has given us all we've had this last week or week and a half this season. This guy has got to be tired, Charlie. Bring somebody in fresh." So Charlie goes back to the dugout and calls the bullpen where this same man, Clyde Sukeforth, was coaching. When he asked Clyde Sukeforth who was throwing the hardest in the bullpen, Clyde turned around and looked and saw Carl Erskine bounce a curve ball in the dirt, and Ralph Branca had just thrown a fast ball, and it looked pretty good to him. So he said Branca was throwing the hardest. So Charlie said, send in Branca. And Branca came in and went onto the mound. And when I got ready to leave the mound, he patted me on the fanny and said, "Don't worry about it, big fella, I'll take care of everything."

Rust: And you took that long walk out to center field.

Newcombe: Yes, but it took Ralph two pitches. And he sure took care of everything . . . but you know I want to add this, Art . . . Ralph Branca has been vilified over the years for that one pitch or two pitches that he threw to Bobby Thomson, the one pitch being that famous home run. But, who set the stage for Ralph Branca?

Who made all that happen? It was the guy who left the

130

tying runs on base, which was Don Newcombe. And Don Newcombe got none of the negative publicity, none of the going over the coals and raking over the coals, as they did to Ralph Branca. I will always remember him coming into the clubhouse after that game was over and sitting on the top landing, the top landing at the Polo Grounds at the clubhouse. I will never forget Ralph sitting with his head down between his legs, crying like a baby, and I said to myself, "My God, is this what baseball does to a guy?" And I had my clothes on already, and I left the clubhouse. I didn't see them anymore for the rest of that year, and the next year I was put in the military.

I always worried about Ralph, and I am still concerned about it. How much of an impact did that have on Ralph Branca? He threw a pitch and somebody hit a home run. . . . So what? No big deal. I've seen home runs hit off some other people before and there were some great pitchers that he hit home runs off of, but nobody ever said "Hey, let's blame Don Newcombe a little bit. He put those tying runs on base and he left them there for Ralph to—you know, to come in and deal with."

Rust: Don, you're a helluva guy. I like the way you said that.

Newcombe: Well, I always worried about Ralph. And I told him that day. I wonder how much of an impact it had on him and his future career, his future life.

Rust: Ah, what was the real story, the truth about the Hotel Chase in the Mound City, in St. Louis? You, Jack Roosevelt Robinson, and Roy Campanella. Jackie said he was going to eat in that dining room and not in his room. What is the real story?

Newcombe: From the beginning, when Jackie first joined the Dodgers in '47, when the team would go to St. Louis, he couldn't stay with his teammates. He had to stay in another hotel. The weather is such an important factor all the time . . . the heat, no air conditioning in our rooms, and we had to eat substandard food, and Jackie had been doing this on his own, in 1947, until Dan Bankhead got there, and later, Roy Campanella, and then myself. But we all had to live under that same configuration. We could not live in the Chase Hotel with our teammates. We had to get off our train in St. Louis and get our own suitcases, find a taxi cab in the mornings, and go to this substandard hotel. The other players on our team would get on an air-conditioned bus; they didn't have to touch their shaving kits unless they wanted to. And they'd go to the Chase Hotel, which was air-conditioned and a beautiful hotel. We could never figure that out. We knew it had to change, but we didn't know just when.

So now 1947 to 1954, there's a seven-year span there, and nothing changed up until 1954. As I mentioned, I went into the military in '52 and '53 to fight for my country. I didn't go to Korea, but it took two years out of my career. When I came back from the military, I rejoined the Dodgers. I said to Jackie one day in St. Louis when we got there, I said, "Jackie, I'm not going to live like this any longer. I've just spent two years in the Army fighting for my flag, for my country. Whether it was in combat or where it was, I still took those two years out of my life. Now, I'm not going to live like a substandard human being any more unless somebody can tell me just why I've got to live like that. I think we've lived like that long enough."

Jackie said, "Newk, you're right, let's go to the hotel and find out why we can't stay there." We asked Roy if he would go too, but Roy said, "No, I'll stay here until you get back." So Jackie and I got a cab, and we went over to the Chase Hotel. We walked in the front door and found the manager of the hotel. I was there, and I'm telling your listeners, Art, that this is the way it happened.

Don Newcombe

Jackie and I found the manager. He took us into the dining room of the hotel and bought us a cup of coffee, because he was a very generous man. And Jackie said to him, "Listen, do you know why we are here? Don and I want to know something." He said, "Yes, I know why you are here. You want to know why you can't stay in this same hotel with your teammates." As God is my witness, here is what the man said: "The only reason we don't want you staying here, or didn't want you staying here all these years is because we didn't want you using the swimming pool." Jackie said, "My God, what are you talking about?" He said, "I don't even know how to swim." Jackie knew how to do everything, but he didn't want that man to know he knew how to swim. I said, "I don't swim during the baseball season. I'm afraid to hurt my arm." So he said, "Okay, it's all right. You can move in then, but just don't go in the swimming pool."

Art, when we moved into the hotel, he made sure, that manager did, that we never got a chance to even look at the swimming pool, because he put us on the other side of the hotel, away from the swimming pool. So we could never get a chance even to look at what was going on. I don't know what his whole premise was . . . maybe he didn't want us looking at those pretty white women walking around the pool deck with all their bikinis on. But he didn't know me. If I wanted to look at something pretty, something beautiful, I was going to look at it whether he segregated me or not.

Rust: Oh, my. Now where is Campanella while all this is going on?

Newcombe: Campanella stayed at the hotel. He stayed there because Roy was not a kind of guy who would go about the business of trying to change the attitudes of people. Roy was just an easy-going, you know, smooth-going

133

kind of guy, a quiet guy, just doing a job. Jackie was a different kind of man. He was outspoken, and he wasn't going to stand for it. He had stood for it long enough. And he wasn't going to stand for it any longer, nor was I.

Rust: Was that the reason for the break between Jackie and Roy?

Newcombe: That might have been a factor in the whole scheme of things as far as Roy and Jackie as personal friends were concerned, Art, but I don't think that was the determining factor. Because we all eventually moved into the hotel. We all played on the same team. What happened to Jackie and Roy was a personal thing that I am not privy to. So I can't tell you or your listeners exactly what happened.

There are many playing baseball today who have forgotten what Jackie Robinson did, have forgotten what Satchel Paige did, forgotten what Roy Campanella did, and, yes, even what Don Newcombe did. They have forgotten what we have done to make it possible for them. I am very dismayed about that. I hope that somehow, some of the messages can get to these players and change their attitudes about what should be done today, because there are kids following them, and they are going to have to leave some kind of legacy on this earth for the kids to benefit from.

Rust: Peter Ueberroth commemorated Jackie's 40th anniversary in 1987, putting number 42 on every second base and 42 on the arms of every ballplayer in the major leagues.

Newcombe: Yeah, that's all well and good, but I don't think it's enough. I think there needs to be some kind of a movement made to assist the Jackie Robinson Foundation—to make it possible for kids to go to school and learn, and maybe to become athletes like Jackie was. Jackie is my idol, Art, and I will never forget him for what he did for me. And I am telling kids today the same thing. I wouldn't let them forget Jackie Robinson, and I don't think baseball should be allowed to forget him in any way. I am even thinking in terms of a national holiday for Jackie Robinson to somehow keep Jackie in the minds of people, especially the young people, because of the contribution he made.

I will never forget having dinner at my house one night in 1968 with a very, very wonderful, famous man, who sat at my dinner table. And he said, "Don, you and Jackie and Roy will never know how easy you made it for me to do my job." His job was civil rights, and that man happened to be Martin Luther King, Jr. One month later he was killed in Memphis because he had a dream and he believed in something. The same as Jackie believed in something. There Martin Luther King was at the time having dogs put on him and having hoses shot on him, and he was even thrown in jail, and we made it easy for him to do his job—in 1968. Supposing it was Martin doing the same job he did in 1947 like Jackie did, where would Martin Luther King be? Would he have made it to 1968? I doubt it.

10

Mickey Mantle

WHEN I think of Mickey Mantle I think of a guy with raw, Tarzan-like strength. When he hit the ball, it was smitten (past tense of smote).

He was great, and I wonder and marvel about it. I don't know how many times I saw the late New York Yankee trainer, Gus Mauch, tape up Mantle's legs like a mummy before each game. Mantle was a victim of chronic osteomyelitis, a bone inflamation of his left foot. When he was in his first season with the Yankees in 1951, he sustained an injury to his right knee. There has to be something about a man who endured that kind of pain and still came up a winner. I admired his endurance.

——— ▬ ———

Rust: Who had the biggest influence on your career?

Mantle: You know, a lot of guys, like guys that work here in New York and commute back and forth; they don't get to see their kids that much. I was lucky. I had a dad that got home at four o'clock every afternoon and he worked with me from four o'clock till dark every night, and luckily, he knew some stuff about baseball. He was one of the best semipro baseball players down in Oklahoma, so he taught me a lot about baseball. This is for kids, you know—their dads don't get to work with them all that much. And sometimes bad advice can be worse than no advice at all.

Rust: Would you do anything differently in your life?

Mantle: If I had it all to do over, I would take better care of myself.

Rust: Everytime I see you, you know what I think about? The '64 Series, New York Yankees vs. the St. Louis Cardinals. What do you remember about that?

Mantle: When I go around the country, everybody always asks, "What's the biggest thrill you ever had in baseball?" You know, it's really hard. I played more games as a Yankee than anybody, and I hit a lot of World Series home runs and got Most Valuable Player and had the triple crown, but that home run there. . . .

Rust: You hit the hell out of it, off Barney Schultz.

Mantle: It was a well-hit ball.

Rust: Of course, I was a Cardinal fan. I'm impressed, but I'm a Cardinal fan. I died then.

Mantle: Well, you can't win them all, you know. . . .

Rust: You can't win them all. Now, Mickey, who was the toughest pitcher for you?

Mantle: There was an article saying "Did you know that Dick Radatz pitched to Mickey 66 times and he struck him out 44?" So I would have to say that Dick Radatz was the toughest pitcher for me. I didn't even realize that he was. I never used his name before until the other day. Now I do.

Legends

Rust: How about the left-handed pitching, Mick? You were such a great right-handed hitter.

Mantle: Well, I didn't mind anybody left-handed—Sandy Koufax, or any of them. I liked to hit right-handed, and I don't feel that anybody could get me out left-handed or right-handed.

Rust: What about the Denny McLain story?

Mantle: It was my last time up in Detroit in 1968. McLain won 31 games that year. Bill Freehan was catching, and McLain called Freehan out in front of the plate. He was like about ten feet from me and I could hear what he was saying. He said to Freehan, "Let's let him hit one—it's his last trip into Detroit. Everybody'll get a kick out of it." So when Freehan came back I said, "Did he say what I thought he said?" Freehan said, "Yeah, he wants you to hit one." But you know, you don't know what he's—Denny McLain's a little whackey. You don't know if he's gonna let you hit one. So the first pitch he threw, I took it, and he looks at me and, of course, he looks like he's thinking, "Why didn't you swing at that one?" So I thought, okay. I told Freehan, "Is he serious?" And Freehan said, "Yeah, he wants you to hit one." So the next pitch he threw was right down the middle and I swung too hard and popped it up to the back-stop. The next one he got right in the same spot, and I hit it into the upper deck. When I was coming around third base, I looked out at him and he gave me a great big wink and a grin. You know, he was happy. The funniest thing that happened during that incident was with the next hitter, Pepitone—Joe Pepitone. He was walking up to home plate. He took his hand and put it out right over the plate, right where he'd like to have one—and Denny knocked him down.

Rust: You lost that game, I believe, didn't you?

Mantle: Yeah. He had us 6 to 0 at that time. I think they beat us like 6 to 3 or something like that.

Rust: I'd like to ask you about Willie Mays, about the comparisons you guys always had to go through. Was it good, bad—what do you think?

Mantle: Oh, I liked it. What you have to look at is the statistics at the end, and he had a lot better ones than I did. He played for about twenty or twenty-two years, almost injury-free. I feel that there was a couple of years in there when I was going along real good without any injuries or anything. I was then pretty good, about as good as him. But at the end of it you have to look at the bottom line, and he's got the best bottom line.

Rust: Mickey, the injuries all started—I was there when you stepped in that drain.

Mantle: 1951.

Rust: '51—in the second game of the World Series— against the New York Giants at the Yankee Stadium.

Mantle: Willie Mays was leading off the sixth inning for the Giants. I moved a few steps toward DiMaggio in center field. Mays hit a fly ball between Joe and myself. I moved towards the ball and Joe cried out that he had it. I stopped short. My spikes got stuck on the cover of a drain in the outfield grass. I heard a pop from my right knee and down I went. Later, the Yankees' team surgeon, Dr. Sidney Gaynor, removed torn cartilage from my knee. That was it for me and the World Series.

Rust: Did you ever face Satchel Paige or Bob Feller?

Mantle: Yeah, I faced both of them. Both of them were over the hill when I faced them, but they were both great pitchers. Bob Feller, I caught him on about his last two years or his last three or four years. Satchel Paige, when I faced him, must have been about sixty-five years old, but the only way I could hit him was to drag a bunt and outrun it to first base.

Rust: I've got to ask you one question. All the thrills you provided me with all these years, there's one that kind of stands out in my mind. I think it was a game against the Minnesota Twins, and you hit a ground ball to Zoilo Versalles at shortstop. You were running like crazy to first base, and you went down like you were shot. What happened?

Mantle: I pulled the back of the hamstring loose on my left leg. I think I missed about six weeks after that.

Rust: You came back, I think, against Cleveland, and hit a three-run homer?

Mantle: That's right—in Cleveland. We got beat 9 to 8 in that game. My home run put us ahead and I thought we were going to win, but somebody hit a home run off Jim Coates—like Rocky Colavito or somebody like that.

Rust: Mick, when you came up, didn't you wear number six?

Mantle: Well, when I first came up, Bobby Brown was in the service; he was number six. Pete Sheehy, the Yankees' equipment manager—you know they'd been writing all that stuff about how I was gonna be the next Babe Ruth or Joe DiMaggio and Lou Gehrig all rolled into one. So Sheehy gave me number six. He thought that'd be a good idea. Well, when Bobby Brown came back out of the service he wanted the number six back, so they had to give me number seven. Cliff Mapes had number seven and they traded him and gave me that number. I'm glad it happened because I really liked number seven.

Rust: What it amounts to now is that they would have retired number six instead of seven. I think one of the things that made you a great ballplayer in my eyes was your speed and your ability to drag bunt with two strikes on you. How did you develop that?

Mantle: I used to do that a lot if I was in a slump. If I'd go like 0 for 10 or 0 for 12, I used to drag bunt, especially leading off an inning if we were behind. Manager Casey Stengel got to where he didn't like for me to drag bunt too much. And talking about Satchel Paige again, we had a game against him one night, and there was a guy on first base. We were behind by one run and you know, of course, I'm supposed to hit the home run and drive in two runs and win that game. Well, I tried to drag bunt with two strikes on me and I fouled it off—and that was the last out of the game. I never will forget it because when I come back in the dugout nobody moved. Everybody was just sitting there. Nobody could believe that I would try to drag bunt with two outs in the ninth inning and two strikes on me. They asked Satchel Paige—the next day they asked Satchel about that, and he said, "Well, I'd of give Mickey first base if I'd known he wanted it." He was happy that I didn't hit a home run off him. But I used to try to drag bunt on guys whenever I didn't think I could hit 'em.

Rust: When you were first sent down in '51—I know you weren't up for the whole season—I heard that you had a lot of problems in Kansas City getting on base, and didn't you drag bunt at one time?

Mantle: First time up, when they sent me down, the first time up I bunted. George Selkirk was our manager, and he said, "Hey, Mick, we know you can bunt, they didn't send you down here to learn how to bunt. Casey said he wants you to start hitting the ball and getting your confidence back. You've lost all your confidence. He wants you to start hitting the ball and get your confidence back." I didn't get another hit for like twenty-three times at bat.

Rust: Well, you know, I guess the only difference is that Willie Mays stuck around in '51 and worked his way out against Warren Spahn. You just didn't get the same chance. But like I said, because of your speed and because you could drag bunt so well, I thought you had it over him. You didn't see Willie bunt too much.

Mantle: No, he didn't have to. He didn't hit left-handed either. You have to be a left-handed hitter to drag bunt.

Rust: Mick, I'm gonna throw some pitchers' names at you and you tell me what you think of them. Chuck Stobbs.

Mantle: Well, I had good luck against him.

Rust: Down in Washington, DC. Tell us about it.

Mantle: I really liked that park. I hate to keep bringing it up. I know if he's sitting around, he'd say he had to get me out a lot of times. I remember one time after the people at Washington had traded him to the White Sox, and I was hitting with the bases loaded. Al Lopez went out and took out, I think, Dick Donovan, the sinker-ball pitcher who was pretty good. I had trouble with him. And he brought Chuck Stobbs in to pitch to me. I couldn't believe it. I went back and got my right-handed bat, and I come back up to the plate and I'm standing there looking at him. He's warming up. He looked at me and he just kind of shook his head—looked at me like, "Do you believe this, he's got me pitching?" Anyway, I got a home run off of him.

Rust: And you did it again—well, describe the round-tripper in Washington, at Griffith Stadium off of lefty Chuck Stobbs in 1953.

Mickey Mantle

Mantle: Oh, it was—it was probably, I guess, the longest ball I'd ever hit. They measured it at 565 feet, but it was wind-blown. I mean, the wind was behind us that day, and the old Griffith Stadium wasn't as tall as the new ballparks, like Yankee Stadium, so the wind came and helped blow the ball out, and it carried 565 feet. It was my longest home run, hitting right handed.

Rust: What about that left handed shot off Pete Ramos?

Mantle: Well, that—there was a ball hit—I hit the ball in Yankee Stadium—Ramos's ball hit the roof, too. But I hit one off Bill Fisher in a night game one night that I think was the hardest ball I'd ever hit. I'm sure it would have gone over 600 feet if it hadn't hit the facade.

Rust: How would you like to see ball clubs develop pitchers?

Mantle: I like to see teams take young pitchers and develop them. I've seen it done. When he came to the Orioles, Paul Richards brought four young pitchers up and they came off good. The Mets now have four or five young pitchers who are real, real good. I think that's the name of the game.

Rust: Everybody talks about your home runs, but to me you were probably one of the best, if not the best, base runner. The epitome of your base-running ability was the 1960 World Series. In the ninth inning you were down, I think it was two runs, and Yogi hit the ball to the first baseman. Yogi hit the ball and it should have been a double play, and you're the only one that I could even imagine who would have got back to first base and beat the tag and kept the Yankees out of the double play. You kept the Yankees going in that Series when they should have been out of it right then and there. I thought that was just tremendous.

Legends

Mantle: The reason is I hit in front of Yogi for about 10 years, and I knew that he hit a lot of line drives down the first base line, so I'd been trying to do that for a long time.

Rust: When you played, how would you have felt to have a Rickey Henderson up in front of you? But you never had, really, the hitter who would ensure that you'd see fastballs.

Mantle: Well, if you got a guy who can steal second and third, they're gonna try to get the ball over. What I really liked was hitting in front of Yogi. You know, my first 10 years I hit third, but when Roger came along, Ralph Houk put me hitting fourth and Roger third. I think that helped Roger a lot, but hitting third in front of Yogi, and with Elston Howard and those other guys behind you—it was really great. I never knew how good it was until they all retired and quit. In '65, '66, '67, and '68, everybody was gone but me and all they had to do was walk me and we couldn't score. So then I realized how much it meant to have guys like that behind you.

Rust: It took a Roger Maris on the Yankees before the Yankee fans really truly appreciated you. I think prior to Roger's 1961 season when he hit the 61 home runs, the Yankee fans were probably expecting too much from you and probably getting on you much more than they should have. It's unfortunate that it had to take Roger's demise as a Yankee for you to get the recognition that you deserved.

Mantle: I'm with you. I felt bad for Roger, but it seemed like it really did happen just like you said. When Roger beat me in the home run race was when everybody started giving me standing ovations all over the country. It was like they were pulling for me and not pulling for Roger, which was terrible, but it really did seem like that.

Rust: Mick, when you were drinking heavily, did you worry about how that would affect your image?

Mantle: No, when I was doing most of that drinking, I was only about 24 or 25 years old, and I was leading the league every year and I was having a good time. When you're young and going good, you don't realize. I had a lot of guys like Allie Reynolds and Vic Raschi, and even Yogi, Hank Bauer, my old friends, such as Gene Woodling—everybody kept talking, saying things about me and Billy Martin and Whitey Ford, saying if you guys don't slow down, you're going to be over the hill before your time. But we were— like I said, we were young and we didn't realize that we were hurting ourselves, and we just kept going. I really do believe that I could have played a lot longer if I'd have been smarter.

Rust: Also, when you were in the home run race in '61 between you and Roger Maris, did it bother you when there was talk about you and Roger—that you were having problems between you?

Mantle: Well, a little bit because it wasn't true. Any time they write untruths about you, you get mad, but I can remember he used to wake me up in the morning—we roomed together here in New York—and sometimes he would come in and wake me up and bring me a cup of coffee and say, "Hey, you better get up, we're fighting again, according to the newspapers." And you know, we got a kick out of it. But it made me feel kind of funny because people really did believe that we didn't like each other. That made me feel real bad.

Rust: Do you think that you were treated really fairly when you were banned from baseball by Commissioner Bowie Kuhn?

Mantle: Well, I can't yell at Bowie Kuhn because he did what he thought was right. He even sent me a letter before I took the job at the Claridge Hotel that he was going to have to ban me if I took the job. I was forewarned. I can't really be mad at him. The only thing I think he should have done was just exactly what Peter Ueberroth did—come down there and look and see what I do around the hotel. I do more charity work now than I have ever done in my life—I go to Baltimore for the Save the Heart Campaign. I go to Boston for the Jimmy Fund. I go to the Special Olympics with Eunice Shriver Kennedy in Philadelphia. Half of the stuff that I do for the Claridge Hotel is charity work right there. If he would have come down there, if he would have taken the time to come down and check me out just to see what I did down there, I don't think he would ever have banned me in the first place. But he didn't take time to do that.

Rust: Did you resent or did the players resent Jim Bouton getting into their private lives as much as he did in the book *Ball Four*?

Mantle: I didn't read the book, but as far as I'm concerned he did a "no-no." You know, what you say here and what you do here should stay here. That's here within the club-house. I wrote a book, *The Mick*. I don't know if you read it or not, but most everything you read there in that book had me in it. If I wasn't—I mean, he didn't say anything about himself as far as I'm concerned, and I didn't read the book—I didn't like it. I don't like him, and a lot of players don't.

Rust: Well, *Ball Four* shows ball players for what they really are—human beings, just like you and me. The general population going out and having a good time and doing things that people really do.

11

Rod
Carew

*CAREW won seven batting ti-
tles with that great, inside-out swing. It made it almost
impossible to fool him. Rodney stood 6-feet tall and
weighed 175 pounds. He was the picture of fastidiousness
and discipline up at the plate.*

*He simply sprayed the rock. He hit the ball all over
the old orchard. He got on base, stole bases, and scored
runs.*

*As a person, Rodney is ramrod straight. He is quiet
and low-key. Those are my impressions of him. My mother
know his family from Colon, Panama. We're both New
Yorkers of Panamanian descent or, I should say, Americans
of Panamanian descent.*

Rust: Rodney, I'm going to reminisce a little bit, I'm going
to go back to one hell of a year that you had in 1977. Right
off the top of my head, I believe you got at least one bingle
in all but 24 games played with Minnesota, and you flirted
with the .400 mark all season. You finished with a .388
batting percentage, the highest since my guy, Ted, The

147

Legends

Thumper, Williams, had an identical batting average 20 years earlier and the second highest since Williams in 1941 when Ted hit .406. What are your comments, what are your memories of the 1977 season?

Carew: Well, you know, it was a great year. It was one of those Cinderella years that any ballplayer would have enjoyed going through. It seemed that everything that I hit was a base hit. Some days I went out there and I didn't feel well, and I'd get three or four hits, or five hits a ballgame. The baseball started looking like a grapefruit coming up to home plate. It didn't matter who was pitching. It was just something that—I don't know, it was uncanny.

I enjoyed it and I—the toughest part of '77 was handling the press itself, because in every city that I went into there were always people that wanted to do interviews with me. It started distracting me from playing the game. I had to sit down with Gene Mauch one day and tell him that as much as the Minnesota Twins needed the publicity and as much as I would like to have the publicity, to me the most important thing once I get in between the two white lines is to go out and play the game hard. I found that, for instance, in one ballgame we had two outs, and a ground ball was hit to me at first base, and I turned and fired to second base—going for a double play. It happened a couple of times in a couple of ballgames, so I just said I'd get to the ballpark at 3:30 every day and would gladly accommodate anyone who wanted to interview me, but once batting practice started, I didn't really want to be bothered. I was going out to do my job, and that was the most important thing.

Rust: You know, Rod, let's go back—let's go back to 1972 when you won the batting title and you didn't hit one solitary round tripper—not one single home run. Tell us about that.

Rod Carew

Carew: Well, I grew up being a power hitter until I got into professional baseball. Then I adjusted my batting stance, adjusted my bat, and after the '68 season hitting .273, I decided that I wanted to be a .300 hitter. I didn't care too much about hitting ten or fifteen home runs. I knew that the important thing for me was to get on base—to try to score runs and have the other guys drive me in.

So after that season I decided, well, I'm just going to try to hit for a higher average and forget about the home runs. You know, that year I didn't hit any home runs and I took my case to arbitration. And I lost my case because, even though I led the league, the Twins' main point was that I didn't hit any home runs. So I accepted that, and then the following year I went out and I hit six home runs. Just some unforeseen thing happened that year that I hit six home runs. I hit 14 home runs in 1975. The people in the organization knew that if I wanted to go for the long ball . . .

Rust: You could do it.

Carew: In my career, I could have done it.

Rust: Rod, your various batting stances, you would adjust from day to day or from game to game according to the pitcher. Want to talk about that?

Carew: I've been trying to teach youngsters this same type of hitting, not using my batting stances but using different ways during a ballgame. If the pitchers get you out two or three times in your first three at-bats, and if you are in a slump, you should adjust right away. So I experimented right away with maybe five or six different batting stances, and I would change from pitch to pitch or from at-bat to at-bat so that if the occasion came up where I needed to switch right away, I wasn't going to be uncomfortable at all.

You know, in 1977 I faced Ed Figueroa three times and

149

he threw me three sliders that I hit weak ground balls to the second baseman. For the fourth time up, Gene Mauch looked at me and he said, "What are you going to do now?" And I said, "Well, I'm going to open up my stance and when he throws me the slider, I'm going to hit that slider to left center field. Sure enough, the second pitch he threw me was a slider and I hit it out to left center field for a triple. So, you know, I knew what I wanted to do and I made the adjustment and I was comfortable.

Rust: Rodney, let's reminisce again—in 1976, George Brett hit .333, beat out his teammate Hal MacRae by a single point when your outfielder, Steve Brye—you remember that one—of the Minnesota Twins allowed a fly ball to drop safely in Brett's final at bat. You finished two points behind Brett that year. What were your thoughts about that?

Carew: The amazing thing about that is that Gene Mauch told me before the series that if I went 7-for-12, I would win it. Well, I went 7-for-12—and they brought in a special scorer to score that three-game series we were playing. The first ball George Brett hit right at Roy Smalley at shortstop, who booted it, and they gave him a base hit. And I figured it's a hometown boy, you know, and they're going to do everything they can to see that George wins the batting title. But, as far as Steve Brye dropping the ball in the outfield, I saw him . . .

Rust: He didn't drop it, he just let it fall.

Carew: I saw it go back and he put his hand up right away so I knew that the sun, especially in the Kansas City ballpark—the sun in left field is pretty bad out there. I think he lost it for an instant and then he tried to come in and catch it and never made the play. There was a big controversy about it, and Mauch went up to Cookie Rojas and asked Cookie if he thought that Steve had dropped the ball intentionally. Cookie said no, he didn't think that he did—he pointed out that he lost the ball. Cookie was a coach at Kansas City at that time. Hal MacRae thought he told Steve that if Brett hit anything out his way, he should let the ball fall in. I wasn't too concerned about it because I thought that I went out there and did my job . . . you can hope that the pitcher holds the hitter, but if he doesn't, there's not much more that I could have done about it.

Rust: Okay. Rodney, you won seven batting titles. There's no question about that, but in my mind's eye you were an extraordinary batting oddity. That tended to overshadow the fact that you had great base-stealing skills.

Carew: People never really gave me the credit for the way that I played the game. I think they gave me more credit for hitting .350 and .360 every year. I went out and I stole bases and I played the middle game. I moved the runners over and played my position, because to me that's what baseball is all about.

You have the Reggie Jacksons, the Don Baylors, you know, all the great home run hitters who are going to hit the ball out of the park. But you also have to have the guys who can set up the RBI situation for the ballclub if you get behind or if you need to tie a ballgame up or go ahead. So I felt that by doing the little things I was helping my team a lot more than the big guys would.

They never gave me credit for my fielding, and I feel like I'd done a pretty creditable job over the years. I played second base and also played first base. You know, when they talk about Ted Williams, the talk about him being a great hitter, but you never hear about Ted Williams's fielding or base running. It seems that we always get overshadowed in some areas of the game.

Legends

Rust: Ted didn't give a damn about fielding, that was his problem. But, no, he didn't have any problems, really. Of course, you stole home seven times in '69, am I correct?

Carew: That was set up by Billy Martin. We worked on it in spring training, because Billy came up to me and he said, "Rod, some days, you know the hitters might not be hitting, so we're going to work on something—to see if we can steal some runs." And he worked with me as far as timing the pitchers, the wind-up over at third base, getting the good short walk leading off the bag, and breaking—showing me when I should break when the pitcher's getting ready to deliver. So I had a sign with the hitters. They knew that once I flashed that sign, they were not supposed to swing. They were supposed to try to block the catcher out for me so that I could slide under safely.

I did it six consecutive times. The seventh time I did it in Seattle. I knocked the catcher down and knocked the umpire down, but the ball was under the catcher. John Rice got up and called me out. Billy just went crazy because he knew that I had gone ahead and had the seventh steal of home, and that would have broken the record.

Rust: No, you tied it. I think my guy Pete Reiser did it in '46, and you tied it. But that would have been the eighth.

Carew: That would have been the eighth—I'm sorry.

Rust: Listen, you were born where my mother was born in Panama. You came here right after World War II, I guess it was in 1945. You went to my alma mater high school, George Washington, in New York.

Carew: Well, I grew up in Panama. My godmother, the lady that delivered me on the train, was a nurse in a hospital in New York. I was fourteen years old, and she used to come back to Panama to visit. She asked me if I would like to come to the United States and finish my high school education and go on to college. I had baseball in my blood, because I was playing since I was about five years old. I started playing—I tried out for my high school team and my coach told me I wasn't good enough to play. So I went out and I played. I played sandlot baseball right outside of Yankee Stadium in Crotona Park in New York.

Some scouts were out there who were looking after me—I had offers from about six or seven different teams. I decided to go with the Minnesota Twins because they were a newly-established club and I felt that with the turnover of players I would have been able to make it to the big leagues a lot quicker there than I would with the Detroit Tigers or the Boston Red Sox or Chicago White Sox. It was a great experience for me because, you know, I never thought that I would get the opportunity to play after I was told by my high school coach that I wasn't good enough.

Rust: Herb Stein signed you, didn't he?

Carew: Right. Herb Stein followed me all over the place —he was like a guardian angel to me. After he saw me and he liked what he saw, he followed me around and he gave me advice and things like that. He was a real big help to me.

Rust: All right now, for a future Hall of Famer, your career ended rather strangely as far as I was concerned.

Carew: It was strange—a strange way that it ended. I was hoping to come back and play in my twentieth season and probably retire after the 1986 season, but no one seemed to be interested in me. I don't know if it was because of the economic reasons or if it was because the owners were trying to show the other players that we know who Rod Carew is and maybe we're going to do something to get the salaries down. Different things went through my mind.

Legends

Rust: The word is collusion.

Carew: Collusion—right. You know, all that stuff went through my mind, so I just went about my business. I figured if no one calls, I spent nineteen good years in the big leagues. This is going to give me a chance to be with my wife and my three daughters. They're at the age right now where they're growing up. Daddy has to be around. So I felt I wasn't missing anything. I missed it during spring training, but once the season started I was so totally involved in doing more things and traveling with my wife and children, going to school with them, and helping them do homework. I did get a call from the San Francisco Giants, but I had decided that I wasn't going back to baseball.

Rust: Rodney, the toughest pitcher for Rod Carew—who was it?

Carew: Rudy May, I think, had to be one of the toughest guys for me to hit—for some reason. Not because he was a left-hander. I didn't care who was pitching out there, but Rudy hid the ball real well on me. I used to tell Rudy that if he underhanded the ball into home plate. . . .

Rust: You still couldn't hit it.

Carew: He still would get me out, but I also told him—I said I'm going to wait until you get a little bit older, and I'm going to catch up to you. The last couple of years of his career I started to hit him.

Another guy was Ron Guidry. He was tough. The "Gator" just went at you. He had a great slider and a good fastball from right when he first came up. He was tough, not only to Rod Carew, but to some of the other good hitters in the league.

Rust: You just mentioned two portsiders—what about some right-handers who gave you a tough time?

154

Carew: Well, I didn't have that much trouble with too many right-handers, unless they started throwing the off-speed stuff. I just sat and waited on their fastball, because I felt like I could adjust off the fastball. I could adjust to the breaking ball and change-ups and curve balls. Off the fastballs I could adjust—I just didn't want them throwing the fastballs behind me.

Rust: What are you doing now?

Carew: I'm having a great time. I just started working now for a company called the National Collegiate Scouting Bureau. I am going out and evaluating high school players. I think it's a great program, because, going back to the year I was in high school and my coach told me I wasn't good enough to play. . . .

Rust: You never forgot that, huh?

Carew: No, I never did.

Rust: Who was that? Was that Dominick Torpe? Who was the coach there?

Carew: He was Art Flynn.

Rust: Art Flynn was it, huh? I hope that he's listening.

Carew: We became real good friends after that. We talked about it, and he said he was wrong. Well, Art, sometimes you have to give people a second chance. I think the importance of what I am doing right now with the National Collegiate Scouting Bureau is going out and evaluating players—young players—from their first year in high school. And some of the kids—you're going to have your blue chip players. But the kids that no one sees, the kids that are in small schools, that none of the scouts really get a chance to see—they're going to benefit from this.

Rust: Let me ask you this—if you were teaching a kid today the basics of hitting, what would be some of the most important things, like step one . . . ?

Carew: I believe that the first thing that you have to tell a youngster is that he has to have confidence. I think that is the most important thing. If you are working with kids that are ten years—ten, eleven years old, you've got to give them the opportunity to swing the bat. So many coaches nowadays are allowing these youngsters to walk up to home plate, and they are telling them to wait for that good pitch. Well, you know, they take ball one, ball two, ball three, ball four, and they never get the pitch that they are waiting for to hit. Kids are going to learn to be aggressive and learn to have the feeling of swinging the bat if you allow them to swing the bat. I think that's the most important thing for young kids.

Rust: Rodney, at a luncheon in 1979 when Calvin Griffith laid down some racial slurs—and of course the following campaign you were no longer with the ballclub—do you want to talk about this?

Carew: After listening to Calvin, I was pretty upset about some of the remarks that he had made. But later on I went in and sat down and talked to Calvin and he explained the whole situation to me—what went on and the way it was taken out of context. It's funny because at the time I was upset at it, but then I went back to the years when everyone in the Twins organization was saying, "We want Rod Carew to go back out and get some more seasoning, because he's not ready to be in the big leagues," and Mr. Griffith put his foot down and he said, "Rod Carew is going to be my second baseman. I have enough confidence in him. He's got—he only played two years of minor league baseball, but I think that if he comes up here and he learns how to play, he's going to be around for a long time." And he stood in my corner for the years that I was with the Twins, and I will never forget that.

I could go in and talk with him about anything. When I was traded in 1979, he called me into the office and told me that he had this chance to use me next year, and he said that he wanted the chance to make a trade for me. He said that I can go to a club that I am going to be comfortable playing with and where they are going to pay me well, because he couldn't pay me. He couldn't keep me and he couldn't afford to pay me, so you've got to respect a man when he comes out and talks to you in that manner.

Rust: Rodney, what about drugs in baseball? And drug-testing?

Carew: We owe the fans a lot and I think . . . and I may take a lot of heat by making this statement . . . but you know, I'm my own person, and I just feel that we should start . . . we have to clean ourselves up. We have to. Baseball is the American sport and we have to try and keep the sport clean. We have so many kids that are coming up today that want to be major league baseball players. If they see these things happening in a game, some of them might turn away and go into some other profession.

Rust: Rodney, what was your top thrill? Was it the '77 season, or otherwise?

Carew: I think it was getting my first major league base hit. Until you get your first hit and it goes through . . . I mean, you are nervous, you are anxious. People have always said that when you get your first hit you are going to get a lot more, so, after getting my first base hit off Dave McNally on opening day in Baltimore. . . .

Rust: That was '67, right?

Carew: '67—right. I think that was my greatest thrill. I had spent two years in the minor leagues and I had spent two years in Class A baseball, and no one expected me to make the jump so soon. Baltimore had won the World Series the year before, and to be playing against the world champions with some of the best ballplayers on opening day . . . I mean, I was thrilled.

Rust: What did he throw you?

Carew: He threw me a slider—I hit a slider—it was down, right up the middle; it went just right through his legs for a base hit.

Rust: Ah, Rodney, the designated hitter. Your feelings about that?

Carew: I think it's great, Art. I think it's great that you're not really taking that much away from the game. A manager is still using the same strategy with the pitcher that he has to do. I think it is going to allow more offense. I think it's going to give a player that cannot go out and play a position a chance to still help the ballclub by going up there often to maybe drive in runs and help the team win ballgames.

12

Ferguson Jenkins

*F*ERGUSON *Jenkins was tall
and a hard thrower with superb control who won 264 games
in his 17-year major league career. The guy threw very
small baseballs.*

Rust: How happy are you for "Pops" getting into the Hall of Fame?

Jenkins: Well, when fellows you played against, like Willie Stargell, get the opportunity to go into the Hall of Fame, it's great. He deserves it; he played well for Pittsburgh. He played like twenty years in their organization, and he was a class individual.

Rust: For the uninitiated, you started with the Phillies in '65. How did it all happen for a guy from Chatham, Ontario?

Jenkins: Well, I was scouted by the Detroit Tigers.

Rust: Well, you're close to Detroit. That figures.

Jenkins: It's only fifty-five minutes.

Legends

Rust: You're right.

Jenkins: I was playing first base at the time. I hit the ball fairly hard, and I had a pretty good arm. A year later, the scout saw me at the age of sixteen. I started pitching then, and I continued pitching until I got out of high school. I got noticed by about eight or nine ballclubs—Boston, Chicago, the Cubs, the Phillies, the White Sox. It just kind of snowballed after Lou DeNunzio had initially told some people about this young fellow up in Canada who was playing baseball.

Rust: You were with the Boston Red Sox for what—'76 through '78; am I correct?

Jenkins: Yeah, two years. Through '77.

Rust: You pitched all those day games with the Cubs. Was that tough because the hitters could see the ball better?

Jenkins: Well, I know that during day baseball you see the ball, as you said, much clearer. At night there's kind of a haze on the ball. Sometimes you only see three-quarters of the ball, but I enjoyed pitching in those day games. I enjoyed the heat of the day, because I was raised close to the Great Lakes, and it was a lot of fun.

Rust: Ron Santo of the Cubs. What was he like to play with?

Jenkins: Ronnie was the fiery type of person on the field. He was real feisty. He loved to play the game. Off the field he was really a lot different individual. Kind of mellow. He got with the guys when he had a family barbecue. But Ronnie was a real hard-nosed individual on the field. He won seven or eight gold gloves for the Cubs, and he had about a .275 batting average for the fourteen years that he played with the Chicago Cubs.

160

Rust: What were your memories, your reminiscences of the '69 season, under Leo Durocher?

Jenkins: Well, Leo was a helluva manager. You know, we had some good ballplayers like Ernie Banks, Billy Williams, Ron Santo, Glen Beckert, Randy Hundley, Kenny Holtzman, Bill Hands. We had a nucleus of about eight or nine fellows who were all the same age, so we could relate to one another. I think that's the nicest thing about playing baseball. The senior player on the team at that time was Ernie Banks, but we were all in our twenties and we enjoyed the game. We enjoyed going to the ballpark and playing, and a lot of times you didn't win. But when you won, that was the delight . . . when you contributed to a win.

Rust: How devastating was it to blow the whole damn thing in 1969?

Jenkins: Well, we got outplayed by the New York Mets. They played sensational ball that last month of September. They won twenty-eight or thirty-some ballgames, and it was a remarkable record. They played about .800 ball, and we just didn't recover from it. We lost a series to Philadelphia, and I think also to the Cardinals and to the Mets. They overtook us. Once we got into second place, we just couldn't recover.

Rust: What's Leo saying while all this is taking place?

Jenkins: Leo wanted to back up a truck—he wanted to get rid of a bunch of guys. He said, "Well, if you guys are that tired, you might as well throw the towel in." But we weren't that tired; we just got outplayed by a lot of good ballclubs that were trying to knock off the winner. They were the spoilers.

Rust: Were you aware that when Tom Seaver lost the Cy Young Award to you that he named his cat after you?

Jenkins: Yeah, I got Tommy pretty good. I heard that he named one of his cats after me—Fergie, Junior, or Fergie something. Tom and I talked quite a bit off the field, and maybe even on it, sometimes just standing behind the bat-ting cages. He was a highly competitive individual, and, let me tell you, whenever I had a chance to pitch against him, I knew I had to have my act together.

Rust: Did you have to make any adjustments to the American League ballparks when you went over there?

Jenkins: The biggest adjustment I had to make was basically with the umpires. I know that they still have that inflated chest protector, and I didn't get the low strikes the first month or so in that first year with the Texas Rangers.

Rust: They can't get down low enough to call it.

Jenkins: Yes, it was just that they were restricted from seeing the low pitch. I had a lot of the umpires say, "Fergie, that's not a strike." And I said, "Hey, I survived in the National League for twelve years pitching down. I'm not going to change it now, because if I come up, I'm gonna get hurt." After a while the umpires started to call that pitch that was down and away or down in the strike zone, and after that I didn't have any problem at all. And the other thing I'd like to tell you about is that in the American League I had the opportunity to face some of my idols. Al Kaline, Harmon Killebrew, and Tony Olivia—some of the older players that were in the American League.

Rust: Going back to the National League, how was the morale of the Cubs in September of 1969 when the Mets started gaining on you?

Jenkins: Well, the morale was still good, although we were watching them in the press and on the scoreboard. We were going into Philadelphia at the time, and we were like two-and-a-half games in front. We lost the series to Philadelphia; I think we dropped about three games in a row. The Mets were half a game behind. We went from Philadelphia into New York. It was like a do-and-die series for us. We lost three straight. Tom Seaver beat us, and Jerry Koosman. The morale was still fairly high knowing that we had to play our own division, but we just didn't have the firepower. Their pitching was just a little superior to ours. I think that's what won the series for them. They ended up finally winning the World Series.

Rust: I was surprised at that time, because I thought the Cubs had a really good ballclub. They just couldn't seem to pull it out.

Jenkins: Well, we had Bill Hands and Holtzman. There was me, and I think Rich Nye as starters. Unfortunately, we didn't score enough runs, and we didn't play enough good ball. The end result is that we ended up in second place.

Rust: Which batter did you fear the most?

Jenkins: Oh, I didn't fear any of the batters; I didn't have a lot of problems. I think that the guy that probably hit me the best was Don Pavletich. He was with the Cincinnati Red Legs at the time. He was a back-up catcher to Johnny Bench, and whenever there was a pinch hitter needed, he was the guy who was put in the lineup. If I was pitching in the second game of a double header, I knew for sure he would be catching. I had good success against guys like Mays and Aaron, Pete Rose, and Rusty Staub. I gave up my share of hits, there is no doubt about that. But I think Don Pavletich probably hit me the best of anybody.

Rust: Was there much pressure on you after you threw six consecutive twenty-game seasons?

Legends

Jenkins: No, I don't really think so. You know, the biggest thing is that everybody expected me to win twenty games for years and years and years. I did it like three, four, five, or six years in a row, but then it came to the seventh year. The Cubs thought my arm was gone. I ended up, I think, 14-and-16. The next year I got traded to Texas in the American League. They were last in their division. I won twenty-five games, so I proved to the people that they were all wrong. There were a lot of reporters who said I had hurt my arm, that my back was gone, or something to that effect. But I kind of discounted that when I ended up winning twenty-five games the following year.

Rust: Fergie, what kind of a toll does it take on players who play for the Cubs? Does it get boring by the end of the season, playing day games all the time?

Jenkins: Well, it becomes boring if you are losing. The number one thing is that the enthusiasm is only brought about if you are having a pretty good season. Now, if you are 4-and-15 or 4-and-12, or you're hitting .220, it's going to be a long season. A lot of times I was very lucky. We had some good players. Billy Williams always hit well, and so did Ron Santo and Ernie Banks. And Kenny Holtzman and I were pitching pretty good. What we were trying to do was to round out the season to make it a good year so we could re-negotiate. There weren't many Cub players who had two- or three-year contracts like they give out now. You signed from year to year, so the incentive was to play well the whole season, the whole 162 games.

Rust: Being a citizen of Canada, how much opportunity did you get as a kid to participate in baseball? Do they really play that much up in Canada?

Jenkins: Well, I started playing at the age of nine. We had service clubs there, like the Rotary, the JCs, Legion ball. I played in leagues like that. I was a first baseman and out-fielder because my dad had played in the outfield. After a while, after I started growing, they put the tall kid at first base. I didn't start to pitch until I was, oh, late fifteen or sixteen years old. Then I started reading up on different pitches and watching people pitch. I was really interested in that. My idol was Larry Doby, with Cleveland at the time. I wanted to be a first baseman. I had pretty good size. When I started to throw or pitch the ball, I had good control. I can't even recollect ever having had a wild ballgame when I started pitching—even as a kid. I threw the ball pretty straight, and I was around the strike zone.

Rust: What was the reason you gave up so many hits in your career?

Jenkins: Probably, similar to Robin Roberts or some other good pitchers such as Seaver. Always throwing strikes. The main thing is that we didn't walk a lot of people. That was the number one factor. When you are a pitcher, you have to be around the plate setting the hitters up, throwing pitches that are called strikes. One result is that sometimes you do get hit hard.

Rust: Did you come up as a relief pitcher, or did they just put you in relief?

Jenkins: I was a relief pitcher with the Philadelphia or-ganization in Little Rock, Arkansas. When I came up in '64 I didn't pitch. I sat on the bench. Then in '65 I came up again and I got the opportunity to pitch. In '64 they were going for the pennant. I was one of the players who thought I could play. I threw batting practice, and then I had to sit in the stands because I wasn't on the roster.

Rust: If you knew then what you know now, would you have been satisfied to be a relief pitcher? Or did you really want to start?

Legends

Jenkins: Well, the Philadelphia organization was grooming me to be a relief pitcher, and that is basically what I did in Double A and Triple A. I was able to come in and throw strikes—that was the big thing. The organization thought that I could help the ballclub. I came in; I wasn't wild; I threw strikes, either a slider, a curveball, or whatever, and the thing is, it was always tight. There were always men in scoring position, and I could throw strikes, either getting a ground ball, or a pop up, or something. Then I left Philadelphia and came to Chicago. I was in a lot of games with the Cubs in relief in my first year in '66. In '67 I won the starting job. Once I won that job as a starter, it enhanced my ability to do certain things, and I could them make more money.

Rust: If I said to you, "Well, here's the money. Let's start a franchise." Who would your starters be?

Jenkins: From the time that I played?

Rust: Yeah, of course.

Jenkins: Well, in right field, I've got to have Roberto Clemente; left field, Hank Aaron; center field, Willie Mays; first base, Tony Perez—that leaves off Willie Stargell, of course.

Rust: That's the way it goes.

Jenkins: Johnny Bench is my catcher; Ron Santo at third; Don Kessinger at shortstop; Joe Morgan at second.

Rust: And who are your pitchers?

Jenkins: Well, Tom Seaver, Steve Carlton, Bob Gibson, Don Drysdale, Sandy Koufax.

Rust: I'll print my World Series tickets right now.

Jenkins: There's a lot of talent that I left off, too.

Ferguson Jenkins

Rust: Who's the manager, or do you need one?

Jenkins: Billy Martin.

Rust: Billy? Why Billy?

Jenkins: Well, Billy Martin was the type of guy who judged people on their talents. He used to always say, "You give me two-and-a-half hours of hard work and I won't ever bother you." That's the kind of rapport he had with a lot of fellows. If you cheated him, the front office, or yourself, he'd always get on you.

Rust: In other words, if you put out, Billy was fair.

Jenkins: Billy—hey, he'd never refute your ability if you put out.

Rust: How do you compare Billy to Leo Ernest Durocher —similar or different?

Jenkins: Similar. I think that Leo was the type of manager that used to always say, "Hey, you play hard for me, I won't ever bother you." Leo was the type of guy who used very few words unless he really got flamboyant. That would be in the dressing room, but he wouldn't ridicule you on the field. He'd wait and get you behind closed doors. But he could judge the talent.

Rust: I want to take you back to the beginning of your major league career, to the '64 Phillies. Do you have any memories that you can relate?

Jenkins: Well, we had some good talent. We had Dick Allen playing third base, Jim Bunning, Chris Short, Art Mahaffey, Johnny Klippstein, and a bunch of good pitchers. We had some guys like Gary Kroll. Ray Culp was a rookie that year. Wes Covington, Johnny Callison—there were so many good, young, talented ballplayers.

Legends

Rust: What was it like to be on a team at the beginning of your career that just went down the tubes like that?

Jenkins: The guys that I came up with were relatively young. For that last month of the season, though, we had about a six-game or an eight-game lead, and then lost it. It's kind of disheartening. I was only twenty years old at the time. I just wanted to say, "Hey, I can do the job if you'd just let me." But we ended up losing like eleven or twelve in a row, and the last game we won, we beat Cincinnati about 10-2.

Rust: What are your memories of playing with or facing Dick Allen?

Jenkins: Dick and I were roommates at Williamsport, Pennsylvania, in Class A. Then we were roommates again when we played at Little Rock. The guy was a super talent. He was very strong. I played against him when he was with the Cardinals, the Dodgers, and the White Sox. Let me tell you, I gave him all the respect in the world when he came to the plate. He was just as dangerous as guys like Pete Rose, Willie Mays, Hank Aaron, Mickey Mantle, or Roger Maris. I think that he had that type of talent. If you made a mistake, he would take you out of the ballpark.

Rust: Fergie, what did you think of Jerry Grote?

Jenkins: Well, you know a ballclub is only as strong as its catcher, and Jerry Grote did an admirable job in the years that he played with the Mets. He got his share of hits off of the Cubs and off me, so I tip my hat to him. He was a good athlete and a good ballplayer.

Rust: We have to mention Koufax.

Jenkins: I pitched against him twice in my career, and that was probably twice too often. Both times he beat me.

Ferguson Jenkins

Rust: How do you think free agency has changed the game?

Jenkins: It has changed the game drastically, because fellows nowadays play two years and then they play their option out. If they're dissatisfied with the ballclub, they can shop around or have their agents shop around and go to a ballclub that's a little stronger, or that they just want to go to for a higher salary. So, what it does is sometimes give one or two ballclubs in a division a nucleus of the power hitters or the best pitchers.

Rust: Would you agree that it is taking loyalty out of the game?

Jenkins: Yes, I think that it does. When I first signed with the Phillies I was hoping to come up and play quite a few years with them, but unfortunately I got traded. Nowadays a fellow can get signed by Oakland, play one or two years and say, "Heck, I want to play in my home state of Missouri. I want to play with the Cardinals or maybe in Kansas City." So that's where the agent says he wants to get traded. Or he goes to where the strong teams are, like Steinbrenner in New York, or up in Boston. It really depends on what your agent has going for you.

Rust: Do you think it's going to last?

Jenkins: Well, it's been in existence about eight years now, and I think before too long football, basketball, and hockey will all have it. I don't think it's going to leave for awhile.

Rust: Do you think you would have gone that route if you had had the opportunity?

Jenkins: Well, I think the Cubs would have probably kept me, but after my second or third year of winning twenty games, it would probably have upped my salary a lot. But I never had the opportunity to do it.

Rust: Back to some other ballplayers. How about Willie Mays?

Jenkins: Well, with Willie Mays, I tried to pitch hard in and then hard away. But the man deserved the respect of every pitcher who ever was in baseball. Let me tell you, that dynamic hitter hit 660 home runs, so you got to give him a lot of respect.

Rust: Hank Aaron.

Jenkins: Hank Aaron. I was very, very lucky against Hank. I think he hit only one or maybe two home runs off me. I pitched him down and in and breaking balls, and I was real successful in Wrigley Field and in County Stadium in Milwaukee and in Atlanta.

Rust: Did you pitch against Mantle?

Jenkins: Just in the World Series competition. I struck him out in one World Series. I think he popped out against me in the other series, but I struck him out in 1967 in Anaheim. And the following year, in '69, or in '68, I think he grounded out to first. I am not sure who was playing first base at the time. I think it was probably McCovey.

Rust: Willie Stargell.

Jenkins: Ah, Willie. I had a lot of good success against Willie. I can't say how many home runs he might have hit against me, but I had good success against Pittsburgh in general. Roberto Clemente gave me all the problems there.

Rust: Do you remember Randy Hundley?

Jenkins: Randy Hundley was one of the first one-handed catchers in baseball. Unfortunately, he had a couple of bad collisions at the plate and they cut his career short. He was the type of guy that, you know, you agreed with him. We used to go over the teams before ballgames, and he would call such a good ballgame. Very seldom did I have to shake him off. He had some good seasons with the bat, and for a while there he was just like Jerry Grote. He was one of the best defensive catchers, and he could throw out a lot of runners—guys like Maury Wills or Lou Brock.

Rust: How about Ron Santo, Don Kessinger, Glen Beckert . . . ?

Jenkins: Well, those guys were all all-stars when I played there. Beckert was an all-star second baseman with the Cubs, and Kessinger patented the jump-throw play from deep shortstop. He was six-three, an all-American at Mississippi. He had some good talent. Ron Santo always had twenty-five-plus home runs and always had close to a hundred RBIs every year.

Rust: And how about the man out in left field?

Jenkins: Oh, we had Billy Williams out there.

Rust: That's the man.

Jenkins: Billy Williams. He just got put in the Hall of Fame last year. Unfortunately, it was a few years later than he wanted, but let me tell you, Billy had a .295 career average, and he hit over four hundred home runs.

Rust: Thanks for the memories, Fergie.

13

Mike Schmidt

I'VE *seen a lot of third base-men with super ability through the last fifty years . . . Red Rolfe, George Kell, Kenny Keltner, Pinky Higgins, Billy Cox, Clete and Ken Boyer, Brooks Robinson, Aurelio Rodriguez, and Graig Nettles. I don't know if any of them could match the all-around ability of Mike Schmidt.*

Schmidt came up in 1972 and established himself as the premier third-sacker of his and perhaps any era. I mean in swinging the bat, fielding, or running the bases. Mike is brilliant in every phase of the game. I'll never forget his 1980 season, when he led the Phillies to the National League pennant and victory in the World Series. He led the league in home runs with forty-eight and RBIs with 121 while batting .286. He was the league's MVP, the first unanimous selection since Orlando Cepeda in 1967.

From several meetings with Mike Schmidt, I'd say that he is introspective and a sensitive human being. Yet he's also one of baseball's most quotable and cooperative players in dealing with the news media.

Mike Schmidt

Rust: Let me ask you a question. How did you become a member of the Philadelphia organization? I know you played at Ohio University.

Schmidt: Oh, just basically the same route that most ballplayers today use to get to the major leagues or into professional baseball, and that was through the free-agent drafting. I was scouted at Ohio, at Ohio University in the Mid-America Conference, and I was picked No. 2 by the Phillies back in 1971. I was a shortstop and they sent me directly to their Double A affiliate, which is at Reading, Pennsylvania. At the end of the next year, they called me up to Philadelphia, and I spent the last month out there then. That's when my career started.

Rust: All right—off the top of my head—you had a brief cup of java in '72, I guess it was, and in '73 it was your first full campaign with the ballclub?

Schmidt: Yup.

Rust: When I say 1980, what do you think?

Schmidt: Well, that was the year Philadelphia will never forget. In fact, when you talk some of the sports, that was the year that they said that Philadelphia was the "City of Winners"—sort of like New York is right now. I think we had an NBA final that year. We had a Super Bowl appearance by the Eagles that year, a world championship by the Phillies, and a Stanley Cup appearance by the Flyers. So that was a really big year for the town of Philadelphia, and obviously, for me as well.

Rust: For the uninitiated, what did you do in 1980?

Schmidt: Well, 1980 was a pretty solid year all the way around. The Phillies won the division and I was elected the Most Valuable Player that year. We got into the World Series against the Kansas City Royals, and I was elected the Most Valuable Player in the World Series, so you might say I had a "hat trick" that year.

173

Legends

Rust: All right, listen, in '76—in friendly Wrigley Field, you hit four round trippers. What are your memories of that day?

Schmidt: I remember it vividly. You remember the name of Dick Allen? I'm sure you do. He made a resurgence back into baseball after sitting out for a year or two.

Rust: You mean the crazy guy?

Schmidt: Ah, you know, it depends. . . .

Rust: The strange one. . . .

Schmidt: But, Dick . . . he did some things that I didn't necessarily condone . . . he became a good friend and an influence on my career, for certain, one day in particular.

    The first thing I remember, now that you mention it, was Dick Allen. He and I sitting alone in the clubhouse. He had asked me to stay behind and he really gave me a real solid man-to-man talk about some things that I needed to hear. He said, "Look, you know, you and I want to go out this door, and we are going to have a ball today. We are going to mess around between innings. We are gonna smile. We're gonna have a good time. We're gonna get back into having fun in this game." And about five hours later, I had me four home runs, a 5-for-6 day, and eight RBIs, and we'd won, 14-13 in 11 innings.

Rust: Who did you pop your round trippers off, Mike?

Schmidt: I believe Rick Reuschel, who is still in the league now and plays for the Giants. At the time he played for the Chicago Cubs. He had a brother by the name of Paul Reuschel, too. And I think the fourth one was off him. Then there was a guy by the name of Mike Garman, who spent some time with the Dodgers and St. Louis and the Cubs, and I forget who the other one was off. I think both the first two were maybe off Rick Reuschel, so I had a pretty good day, and Rick Reuschel is the only one of the three who survived.

Rust: All right, check my memory now—in '79 or thereabouts, you made a radical batting adjustment. You moved away from the dish, closer to the rear of the batter's box. Well, why did you do that?

Schmidt: It's very simple and unlike what young kids in high school and college might realize at this point in their career. But it is something that they would realize once they moved up in baseball. There is a difference. The big difference between higher level baseball and amateur baseball is the ability of the major league pitcher to pitch the ball inside, that is, to throw the ball in on the hitter's hands when he wanted to. I spent years, you know, surviving. I have pretty good credentials to prove I had a few pretty good years up to that point, and I had just got totally stymied by that inside pitch on my hands, to the point where I was consistently opening up my shoulder. I would hit home runs foul, and hit them all foul.

What that did was to make me so vulnerable to that breaking ball that after they threw that breaking ball in on my hands a few times, one game I said to myself, "Look, I want to try something, this other stuff isn't working." So I backed up about a foot in the batter's box from where I originally stood, and the plate was way out there. I could barely reach the outside corner from there, bent over a lot, like you see George Brett and you see a lot of the modern-day hitters. Now adopting that style of standing 'way up from the plate and sort of striding into the pitcher or into home plate. . . .

Rust: That's Charlie Lau stuff.

Schmidt: To a tee. It's the Charlie Lau stuff, it's his style of hitting, and it really frees up the inside corner. You don't have to be so conscious of getting jammed and breaking your bat. In '80 and '81 I had the MVP years and I think that was a big stepping stone in the middle of my career to help me get to the point where I am now.

Rust: Now, you know, Michael, because of your nonchalance and your unemotional demeanor, may I put it that way, you have been the target of a lot of fans' criticism. What do you think about that?

Schmidt: Art, there is no question that throughout most of my career I have had to bow for every ounce of appreciation that I have ever gotten down here in Philadelphia and I think that is the big reason for it. It's not necessarily that I don't try hard, obviously, it's just . . . my dad. My dad is a very unemotional guy and my mother's not too emotional. I've seen my dad sit down in Riverfront Stadium in Cincinnati and watch me hit two home runs in a game three or four times, and he'd hardly clap his hands, you know. He'd just sit there with a look of confidence on his face. But my mom is standing up beating the heck out of him and everybody around. She is cheering, and he's, you know, ho-hum, no big deal. He's been a poker-face Brett Maverick kind of guy his whole career, and I guess that's where I got that way. I feel like I never want the opposition to know what I'm thinking, or whether they got the best of me, or whether I got the best of them. I've always been the kind of guy to stay on an even keel all the time and not get too emotional. I think that the fans have translated that over the years. I think really I have just been under control emotionally most of my career, and I think that that has helped me to get to the point that I am. The big thing about this past year is that the fans of Philadelphia and maybe all of baseball now have come to respect me. It's a really warm feeling for me now in Philadelphia, and a really comfortable feeling for me now to play ball there. And believe me, that's something that I am going to consider when I think about hanging them up.

Mike Schmidt

Rust: From '72 to the present, who were the toughest pitchers for Mike Schmidt? Obviously, there were not too many of them, but. . . .

Schmidt: I could name you a few over the years. When I was a young kid, guys like Tom Seaver. He really could make me look awfully bad with his fastballs over the plate inside and the hard slider away. Of course, he made a lot of hitters look bad. But I always mention Tom Seaver as a guy who gave me the most trouble early in my career. As the years went on, there's always the people down in Houston—God rest his soul, Don Wilson—that pitching staff down there has always had some tough people. Like Nolan Ryan, the guy who I always like to miss when we go to Houston for a series. I kinda hope that he pitches the day before we get there.

Rust: Maybe come up with a stomach ache?

Schmidt: Yeah, Mike Scott isn't that kind of pitcher, but Mike Scott gets you out just as much, if not more. But he's not that uncomfortable to face up at home plate. Mike Scott might be the best pitcher in baseball right now, but I would much rather face Mike Scott than I would Nolan Ryan or a Dwight Gooden, just because of the intimidation factor. Of course, over the years there have been some relievers that have been awful tough. Goose Gossage is an awfully tough pitcher, and I don't look forward to batting against Lee Smith. You know, those are the tough ones. St. Louis has got a kid now by the name of Todd Worrell and. . . .

Rust: Oh, he throws a very small baseball.

Schmidt: Oh, yes, let me tell you nowadays, the 92- or 93-mile-an-hour fastball is the normal pitch. Ten years ago, there might have been one guy on a staff that could rush it up there and get it up there at 93, only because he was wild. Now they got control at 93 or 94 miles-an-hour pitches.

Legends

You know, it's good that this is all happening right at the end of my career.

Rust: Warren Spahn said there are a lot of pitchers who don't throw inside any more, and I was wondering, Mike, which pitchers have you faced this year or last year that have challenged you inside?

Schmidt: Well, there's some truth in what Warren said . . . The game basically isn't anywhere near as intimidating or as "mean" as it used to be. I mean, a couple of players went on their backs every game ten or fifteen years ago, and there were pitchers who were notorious for knocking guys down. As I remember it, Drysdale supposedly was a pretty mean guy out on the mound.

Rust: What about Gibby?

Schmidt: Oh, yeah, Bob Gibson, without question, was one. And I faced Bob Gibson. He was one of the most intimidating men who ever stood on the mound. He would hit you in the ribs in a second, you know, just in a gnat's eyelash. He would hit you if the situation warranted it. And you know, if you don't like it, come on out to the mound and let's see what you want to do about it. That's the way it used to be. There will be instances in modern-day baseball where there'll be retaliation, and there'll be pitches inside and a hitter might get knocked down, but they'll be few and far between. A lot of that has to do with the rules that are in baseball now on the knockdown pitch and the control that the umpires have. Basically, just sort of lackadaisical, the you-don't-hit-me, I-won't-hit-you sort of approach to the game. I don't necessarily go along with that.

Over the years, I think that the ability to pitch inside has become a lost art. A guy like Don Sutton—here's a guy who won 300 ballgames, and pitching that high fastball inside was one big reason.

Mike Schmidt

Rust: In 1980, Mike, in the World Series against Kansas City, I was wondering what ran through your head at third base when Tug McGraw was making that final pitch to Willie Wilson?

Schmidt: Well, that was one of those years. Nothing came easy for us. You always seemed to think that as it had earlier in the playoffs and the World Series, something was going to go wrong. But Tug came through and struck out Willie Wilson and it was all over with. You know, with the horses and the dogs all along the field there in Philadelphia, it was one of the memorable scenes in World Series history.

Rust: But nobody went on the field, though.

Schmidt: I believe that was Mayor Rizzo's influence at the time. They weren't about to let things get out of hand there at Veterans' Stadium. An attempt was made to do that in New York, if I'm not mistaken, but they weren't able to handle it. New Yorkers are hard to deal with when it comes to tearing up that stadium.

Rust: Mike, your thoughts on inter-league play. Wouldn't that pack the ballparks?

Schmidt: No, not necessarily. I think that would wear thin. The mystique of the All-Star Game and the World Series is enough. Baseball has survived the test of time now for, what, almost a 100 years, or way over a 100 years, or whatever it is.

Rust: That doesn't mean you can't change it, Michael.

Schmidt: Well, that's true, but, Art, I don't see a need for that change right now. You know, baseball is—every year I make this statement—baseball is once again at an all-time high as far as the fan appeal, and . . .

179

Legends

Rust: Michael, can you imagine a New York City rivalry between the Mets and the Yankees playing each other?

Schmidt: Yeah, but if it became commonplace, you wouldn't have that for real. If the Yankees and the Mets met 14 times a year, people would get sick of seeing these two teams play each other.

Rust: Well, okay, if that's how you think.

Schmidt: Every team in baseball drew over a million this year. So why do we want to mess with it?

Rust: Michael, you're a traditionalist.

14

Dave
Winfield

THE *man is just one superb athlete. A superb, all-around athlete. He can hit for power, run like the wind, and can catch anything hit his way. He's got a howitzer for an arm. And he gives his all day in and day out.*

He's one of the finest defensive outfielders in baseball. He can throw with most anyone. I love how he runs the bases with 110-percent aggressiveness. He has worn the Yankee pinstripes with dignity.

Personally, I find Dave to be a highly sensitive individual. In my greatest moment of devastation, the loss of my wife, Edna, he rallied around me with a great deal of empathy and understanding. For that alone, I'll never forget him.

Rust: David, let's take it from the genesis—the beginning of Dave Winfield's baseball career. How did you get into baseball? Let's just start from elementary school on.

Winfield: Well, I'll try to summarize things as well as I can. I was eight years old when I started. I had a cousin playing baseball, and my brother got to playing, and we had a recreation center a half block from my house. So it was something for me to get interested in athletics. The focus at that time was largely baseball. They had basketball and football, but baseball was pretty much the organized thing.

Rust: This was in Minnesota?

Winfield: Yes. I played there for my whole life—Little League, you know, midgets, juniors, high school, National League Juniors. Then I went to college at the University of Minnesota, and I played semi-pro ball in Alaska for the Alaska Gold Panners, in Fairbanks. I learned a lot of stuff there. From the time I started I was a third baseman, a shortstop, and then a shortstop and pitcher. By the way, when I was in high school and college, I was a pitcher. I also played a little bit of outfield. When I turned pro, they wanted me to play the outfield. They wanted me to play every day.

Rust: You were drafted by how many other professional ball clubs?

Winfield: Three other professional clubs in two other leagues. We had the Atlanta Hawks and the Utah Stars, who were in the ABA at the time, and the Minnesota Vikings— tight end. I didn't play much football in my time.

Rust: Why did you pick baseball?

Winfield: That's what I always wanted. That's the sport that I played the most. Once I got to college, even though I liked those basketball conferences more than the others, they let me play baseball because I could have longevity. I won't say I was guaranteed of making it or staying in it, but I was pretty confident that that was the case. And it turned out to be that way. This is my 14th season in baseball. How many could you do in basketball?

Dave Winfield

Rust: David, how can you assess, as a black athlete . . . how would you assess your major league career, with all the B.S. and stuff going on?

Winfield: It has been a good career. I can honestly say it hasn't been easy. Anybody who says it's been easy . . . I may make it look easy on the field, but they don't know what goes on behind the scenes and in the locker room and in the board rooms—negotiating and all these kinds of things. It hasn't been easy, and I think the asset that I had going for me is that I was fortunate to have one or two guys in the major leagues that would give me some good advice.

Rust: Who was that?

Winfield: A guy like Willie McCovey meant a lot to me because he is a man on the field and off the field. I learned a lot from him. And I talked to successful people in the game, both black and white.

Rust: Do you want to give any names?

Winfield: We have to go to the Joe Morgans, Lou Brocks, and Hank Aarons—the people like that that I learned a lot from. They are just the ballplayers, the quality ballplayers that I thought had a good reputation, good demeanor, good character—these are the guys that I would try to take a little bit from. They're the ones I learned something from, because in San Diego we didn't have a whole lot of people who were willing to lend advice and offer services. They were fighting for their jobs. I went to Wichita and there I learned a lot. I traveled a lot, had different experiences so I wasn't overwhelmed when I came to the major league level. I think that I have a good family and friends, support—all those character things helped; and my mentor, the guy who turned out to be my agent, David Al Frohman—he helped quite a bit. He'd say go there, do this, try this.

Legends

Rust: He gave you direction.

Winfield: Oh, yeah, really, and he gave me the reasons why, not just telling me to do something or asking me to do something. We spent thousands of hours together and his input was invaluable. When we would negotiate a contract, it wasn't someone just going off and representing me and saying, "Wait two hours and when I come back it'll be over." I was there, not only in there at the happening, but we formed the plans before we went in.

And then I think getting involved in union activities, learning from that standpoint, being a player representative and knowing that baseball is a game and a business and a science too. . . . There are the fundamentals that you can learn and apply consistently to a high level of productiveness. You can become better. There are the things such as timing and balance and all that kind of stuff. So when people say that I am just a streak hitter or that I'm a free swinger, it's just the opposite, because I'm thinking even though you can't apply what you know every day, you do different things.

Rust: You do have your plans. You know what you want to do?

Winfield: There aren't that many big guys around that can hit consistently and do these kind of things, so I'm pretty pleased with that.

Rust: How would you describe yourself as a ballplayer? If you could go outside of yourself, how would you describe Dave Winfield?

Winfield: I'll remove myself from myself for a moment. I would be the kind of guy I'd like to play with. That's not one thing, it's a variety of things, but, a very, very substantial ballplayer—that's the best way to say it.

184

Dave Winfield

Rust: You've experienced a lot in the Big Ball Orchard here in the South Bronx with George Steinbrenner. It's been hot. It's been kinda difficult. What do you say about that?

Winfield: It's been more difficult than it ever should have been, because I'm not the kind of guy that creates problems. I'm not the clubhouse lawyer. I'm not the guy who doesn't play hard. I'm not the guy who doesn't get results or has years fluctuating tremendously from year to year. I stay consistent. I can really be acting the fool . . . they gave me the money and I don't have to do anything and I get my money.

But, I have a lot of pride and it's been difficult. It's been hard to pinpoint the reason. I don't know, but it's beyond the game with serious personal kinds of things that go on. I don't intend to argue and fight all the time, but you have to protect yourself and that's what it has come down to for so long. Maybe one or two years in my career, I'll be able to play without the duress and the distractions, which are all unnecessary. And, on top of that, I'm saying I'm the kind of guy that doesn't come in drunk or high. I'm always ready to play. I think it's good to have a guy like that.

Rust: In my point of view, there was a lot of racism when you were battling with Mattingly for the batting title. Will you comment on that?

Winfield: Well, I agree with you. They term it a lot of different things. At some point they could call it racism, but when it comes down to two guys on the same team battling for the same thing, using the manipulative media and people's perceptions, there was a vast difference in the . . . let's say in the amount of encouragement and kind of things that would go from one man to the other.

It was disheartening to listen and be subjected to it, but I suppose we all experience things like this in life. It was rough, it was nasty, and you can really see where people are coming from.

Rust: When the owner, Steinbrenner, says that he made a mistake letting the other guy go, meaning Reggie Jackson, and keeping you . . . that you're not a clutch ballplayer. What do you say to that?

Winfield: If he made a mistake on Reggie, then he made a mistake. It's got nothing to do with me. I don't have to sit here and justify me being a clutch player. We are different kind of players. With Reggie, you love him or hate him because he would either come through and shine tremendously or bust tremendously, but the confidence would always be there and he could produce at the right time, as he did in a lot of post-season games. We haven't been in too many post-season games, so I really can't make that kind of a comparison. If you want to compare the players, I don't know—who would you want on your team? I think you'd want both of us on your team.

You'd want Reggie because he's gonna attract fans and he can give you the big home run that people like so much. But as far as consistency and bigger numbers, I put them on the board every year. I think I'm an all-around ballplayer.

Rust: When all is said and done and your career is over, what would you like to say that Dave Winfield accomplished in the major leagues?

Winfield: In the major leagues—well, I think this is only a stepping stone in life for me—if I play long enough, God willing, may I stay healthy and the people stay supportive, they may say, "Hey, put that dude in the Hall of Fame." I don't think about that . . . I don't really think about that kind of thing. The things I thought about coming into this game is to do the best that I could and don't give anybody any bullshit and don't take any. Hopefully, when you get out of the game, you have got something to show for it.

Rust: David, you and I used to argue because I consider you one helluva defensive ball hawk. I always wanted you to be the middle guy out there in the outfield. Why don't you take it?

Winfield: By the time they wanted me to play center field—because they ran a couple of other guys out of here who couldn't handle it—I was, I don't know, I was 30, yeah, I was about 31 years old, and I weighed about 230 pounds, and I couldn't be running out there. When you keep running out there, your knees get tired from running around in center field. I could play centerfield as well—or better—than most people, but then the batting's going to stop. You know, "Dave Winfield, he's only got about eighteen homers this year; he's down to only eighty-five RBIs; what's the deal?" I'd have to say you ran me to a frazzle—I'd say that if I were in center—it takes a lot out of a person.

Rust: Will this be Dave's last year (1988) in the Big Ball Orchard in the South Bronx?

Winfield: There's a lot of speculation along those lines. I don't see myself going anywhere else, but you never know what will happen if the right offer, the right circumstances come along. But I love New York. I like playing here. It'd be great to have a year or two without the distractions and the garbage. Then you would see what I could do. That would please me as much as anything. I think the people like my performance, and management really does, too, no matter what they say about it. They can't go and get anybody to do the job better—anybody that dedicated. I can understand the business moves to improve the team—if they get two or three or four guys . . . at least a pitcher. I could understand if there were no personal implications, and if it was right for Winfield to go somewhere. It would have to be awfully attractive—more than palatable. The offer would have to be very attractive for me to go anywhere else.

Rust: Does Dave Winfield consider himself a superstar?

Winfield: I don't comment on those things anymore. I let my peers talk about that. But I know, and anybody—these people that come to see me play—they know the answer.

Rust: Good answer.

15

Don Mattingly

WHEN you mention the name Don Mattingly to me, I think about Friday evening, September 6, 1985, in what I call "The Big Ball Orchard in the South Bronx." That's when I saw Don smash a three-run homer in the Yankee fifth to lead them to an 8-4 come-from-behind triumph over the Oakland A's.

I was in the press box with fellow journalist Carl Nesfield when Don smacked the four-bagger. Nesfield banged his fist on the press box table and said, "Damn. Damn. Damn. The SOB is great." Others in the press box just looked at each other with mouths agape. It was as if, with that one blow, Mattingly had put the lid on his greatness. It was as if that round-tripper was confirmation of his stature.

That incident dredged up memories in my mind of an August twenty-fourth night in 1949 when I saw Ray Robinson KO Steve Belloise in round 7 in the same ballpark. When His Sugarship did that, with such perfection, he put the cap on his majesty.

A couple of decades from now, I hope to be at Cooperstown to welcome the sweet swatter from Evansville, Indiana, into the Hall of Fame. So, make room, Joseph Paul DiMaggio, Stanley Frank Musial, and Melvin Thomas Ott.

Legends

Donald Arthur Mattingly will be moving in there eventually.

Don is decent, warm, and extra-sensitive. He always takes the time to talk with you. He's great not only between those white lines but off the field as well.

Rust: Donny, when I saw you at Fort Lauderdale in spring training in 1982, I knew immediately you couldn't miss. You remind me of a cross between the old New York Giants Don "Mandrake" Mueller and the St. Louis Cardinal Stan "The Man" Musial. Where and how did the Mattingly prowess and batting stance come from?

Mattingly: My batting stance has really changed dramatically, I would say, over the last three or four years. I started out trying to hit open, with the open front foot and the back toe that was pointed backwards, and I just kind of leaned a little bit, almost like copying Rod Carew. I had success, you know, in the minor leagues. I started changing a lot more when I started working with Lou (Piniella). That was at the major league camp; I think that was in 1982. It just evolved since then. I seemed to be getting more consistent with it every year. I just feel like I'm getting better with the stance and doing things better mechanically—you know, the whole thing. And understanding myself—what my approach is, what I am doing wrong. I am able to change myself and make the adjustment.

Rust: Let's trace Don Mattingly from Evansville Memorial High School in Evansville, Indiana, where you played baseball, basketball, and football. How did you get into the Yankee organization? Take it from your high school days on.

Don Mattingly

Mattingly: In baseball I was just drafted. I was drafted in the nineteenth round by the Yankees, and I was signed after the state playoffs in my senior year. And I went on to Oneonta. I've been in the minor leagues, and then the major leagues, ever since then.

Rust: All right, but tell me about high school. What were your ambitions, and what not.

Mattingly: I did okay in school. I got like a B or a B-minus average, but I never really had any intention of . . . I didn't really know what I wanted to do, to tell you the truth, Art. I wanted to play ball and I was always a pretty good athlete. After the scouts came looking at me after my first year in high school . . . ever since then I only wanted to play baseball.

Rust: With Oneonta, you were not the big rock crusher. You were not a big home run hitter. Where does this power come from?

Mattingly: I think the power was coming from me. When I came out of high school, I was 175 pounds. Now I seem to be right around 189–190 pounds, so I have put on 15 pounds and it's not just weight that I have put on. I feel like I have put on strength. I've lifted weights very hard from the time I got into pro baseball.

There are a few things that I think may have helped make me a home run hitter. I will say Lou and the weight shift is probably the biggest reason for me to be able to pull the ball the way I can and as efficiently as I can now. I was never really able to pull the ball as consistently as I can now. I was never able to pull the ball until '82 and '83 when I started pulling the ball in the air. And even then I really couldn't hit the ball out into right center field. If I was to hit a home run it would have to be right down the line.

And now, as I've gotten even stronger and got to know

the pitchers a little more and to know myself, I've started to reach right center, and that makes me a bit more dangerous. And there are a few parks, even in left field . . . like when you go to Seattle and a few places like that . . . When I first went into Seattle I never thought about hitting the ball to left field in the air. If I hit anything to left, I wanted it to be a line drive. I could pull it from there. But now I go into Seattle looking to hit the ball out of the park in left field, and that's the reason you can see the changes.

Rust: Donny, what's the secret of hitting? What's the secret of your hitting? What does concentration have to do with it?

Mattingly: Concentration has a lot to do with it. I think if you can stay tuned into the game—it's not like staying tuned into the game every day for 24 hours—it's a matter of tuning in . . . for me, for three-and-a-half to four hours, or however long you are on the field—that's when you need your concentration. If you hit the ball good, it doesn't matter what you did up there, or what you did all day or all night. It matters what type of concentration you had for the three-and-a-half or four hours during the game.

Rust: Do you adjust to each situation? Do you hit the 'tater—if it calls for a 'tater, if you want to hit the home run—or if you need a bingle, do you get the bingle? What's the Mattingly mystique?

Mattingly: There are times when I will go for a home run. The other night I wasn't really going for the home run . . . all we needed was a base hit to tie the ballgame up. Now, we go into the ninth and the situation where we're down a run, and there's one or two outs . . . I'm going to try to get a pitch I can drive out of the ballpark. I feel like I've got as good a chance as anybody, especially playing in a place like this. If I can be patient enough and wait to get good pitches, you know. In those situations, you can't get hurt to take a couple of strikes. You wait for your pitch and maybe you have to take an outside fastball or an outside breaking ball, but you've got to try and wait and get the guy to come in after you.

Rust: You and Wade Boggs . . . what's the difference between you two?

Mattingly: There're a lot of differences in us and there're a lot of similarities. We both have good concentration. I would say we're both players who are very confident. He's a little more disciplined at home plate. He doesn't swing at too many bad pitches, but he also doesn't try to pull the ball a little harder. He doesn't make many mistakes, and that's why the guy is hitting .370 and .367 a few years, or whatever he's hitting. You don't do that by not being on top of the ball all the time. Myself, I try to pull the ball a little more. I try to do a few more things. Also, he's hitting in the leadoff spot, which is one difference.

I'm hitting in the three hole, where I'm expected to drive runs in. He's trying to get on base for the guy behind him. My job is really to drive runs in and also to get on for the Dave Winfields in our lineup. So I'm a little different in that way as a player, but there's not much difference in both of us besides that.

Rust: Was there any pure animosity, or were there any two factions, one pulling for Mattingly and one pulling for Dave Winfield in the batting race?

Mattingly: I don't think so. If there was, it seems like it was within. Nobody said anything publicly. I know I wanted to stay away from that, and Dave did too. Dave was in a tougher situation than I was. He had been in the big leagues for ten years and had his nice big contract, and he had things his way. I was the guy coming up. I wasn't making any money—you know, the guy that everybody cheers for. He treated it very well, the whole thing. But I have said it a few times, and I'll say it again . . . Dave Winfield really showed a lot of class in that whole situation with me. He handled himself very well the whole time, and I'll never forget that. And that's one thing about the whole race that you want it like this. I'll always remember it with a very special feeling.

Rust: Any pitchers give you any trouble? Give me the names of two or three pitchers who you hate like hell to see on that mound.

Mattingly: Well, Tom Henke is one who is very, very tough to pick up.

Rust: Why is it that he's tough to pick up?

Mattingly: He's tough to pick up. He gets the ball way out on the side from you; he gets the ball basically behind your head. The ball runs in, it runs out. I don't know if he knows where it's going all the time, but he throws hard, too, and everything he throws has good stuff. Everything he throws moves. I mean, I can go through a list of guys who . . .

Rust: Give me some more guys.

Mattingly: Who I'd hate to face in a tough situation? One would be, I would say, Mark Langston from Seattle, and another would be Matt Young from Seattle. Those are two guys that throw very, very hard and also have good breaking balls, and if you don't get a good pitch to hit . . . you may only get one and if you don't hit it, then you can be in trouble.

Rust: You're in New York City. Your first full year here was 1983. How has it been at the Big Ball Orchard in the

South Bronx? I mean, working in chaos? That Steinbrenner, with the B.S. there. How do you play under these conditions?

Mattingly: Well, it goes back to concentration, Arthur. When you talk about how concentration has a lot to do with hitting, well, concentration here has a lot to do with everything. You've got to be able to come out here and throw everything out of the way when you get on the field.

You have to forget about George. You have to be able to forget the city you're playing in. You have to forget about anything that has been written about you and said about you or what anyone thinks about you. You've got to be able to go out for those four hours and play the type of baseball that you know how to play.

And for me that's the easiest thing to do, to come out here and say, okay, forget about everything else. I came to play baseball and that's what I can control. That's the one aspect about this whole city and atmosphere and baseball that I can control. It's the baseball part of it. Nobody can write that. I can't write it, I can't say it, I gotta go out and do it. That's one thing I feel I can control, and that's one thing I try to . . . that I do control.

Rust: Donny, what is, thus far, your No. 1 thrill in the major leagues?

Mattingly: There've been a few that have been that entirely exciting for me because I am so young.

Rust: Eighty-one games in '83, and then ninety-one games.

Mattingly: I was basically platooning in '83. I was playing just against right-handers, and then for me to come back and play against everybody and show that I could hit anybody was a big thrill for me. 1985 was a big thrill for me. I did some things I never thought I could do. I never thought

I could drive in 145 runs or hit thirty-five home runs. I thought I could hit twenty-five or thirty, but I never thought I could be in the thirty-five range, or that I could hit forty all of a sudden. So that's another one that was a big thrill for me.

Rust: What's down the road for Don Mattingly? What would you like to accomplish in your next decade of major league competition?

Mattingly: Well, I'd like to play in some playoff games, Art. That's one thing. And I think we may have a chance to, you know. Right now things look a little bit down, but we're a ballclub that we know is going to be back. There's a lot of tradition here and a lot of pride. And it's something I didn't know about when I first got here. But now I feel a part of it and I feel like if we can continue to be a good ballclub—and keep trying to improve—we're going to be there.